GrassRoutes Travel

Guide to

OAKLAND

The Soul of the City Next Door

Future Titles:

BackRoutes Series
California Wine Country
Lake Tahoe

GrassRoutes Kids
Bay Area

GrassRoutes Girls
San Francisco
Seattle

City Next Door Series
Portland
Vancouver
Baltimore

GrassRoutes Travel™

OAKLAND
The Soul of the City Next Door
Serena Bartlett
Illustrated by Daniel Ling
Edited by Susan Freeman

GrassRoutes Travel Press, Oakland 94609
Copyright © Serena Bartlett, 2006
Illustrations © Daniel Ling, 2006
All rights reserved. Published 2006
GrassRoutes Travel and the GrassRoutes Travel logo are licensed
trademarks of Serena Bartlett

LIBRARY OF CONGRESS CATALOGING-IN-PUBLICATION DATA
Bartlett, Serena
    GrassRoutes Travel guide to Oakland : the soul of the city next door.
-- 1st ed. -- Oakland, Calif. : GrassRoutes Travel, 2007.
      p. ; cm.
    ISBN-13: 978-0-9791462-0-6
    ISBN-10: 0-9791462-0-8
    Includes index.
1. Oakland (Calif.)--Guidebooks. 2. Oakland (Calif.)--Description
and travel. I. Guide to Oakland.
    F869.O2 G73 2007
    917.94/66--dc22 0701   2006939835

Printed in Canada

Tell me about your discoveries, and check out what's new
at GrassRoutes Travel:
www.grassroutestravel.com
info@grassroutestravel.com

Dedicated to

Khempo Yurmed Tinley Rinpoche for his compassion and commitment to world peace.

"Certainly, travel is more than the seeing of sights; it is a change that goes on, deep and permanent, in the ideas of living."

-Miriam Beard

Table of Contents

Introduction..xi

The GrassRoutes Story.....................................xi

Using GrassRoutes Travel Guides...........................xv

Travel Tips xvi

About Oakland 2

History 2

Climate 7

Maps 8

Transit Information 18

    Getting Here....................................18

    Getting Around..................................20

Serena's Top Picks......................................23

For International Visitors.................................26

Emergencies 28

Calendar 30

Up Early 46

Do Lunch..52

Hang Out 62

Casual Night Out 68

Listen..78

Dress Up 84

Get Inspired 92

Create 98

Explore 104

    East Bay Regional Parks 107

Learn..112

Get Active 118

Buy Me 124

    Shopping Districts 132

Crowds 136
Stay Up Late 138
Pamper 142
Stay In 148
Weekend 152
Volunteer 158
City for Free 164
Lodge 174
    Bed-and-Breakfasts 175
    Homestays 176
    Top End Hotels 177
    Airport Hotels 178
    City Center Accommodations 178
    Nearby Hostels 179
    Camping 180
Nearby 182
Index 195
Our Bios 201

Acknowledgements

Thanks to all the people who have shared their views with me and all the people I've traveled with over the years. First and foremost I would like to thank Daniel Ling for his support, his great contribution to this project, his friendship and his love. Thank you to Susan Freeman, whose time, talent and energy have made this project worthwhile. Thank you to Marjory Luxenberg for believing in me and making this project possible. Thank you to Barbara Weinstock, Robert Shuman, Sheryl and Dan Getman, Leslie and Chris Jones, Carla Lopez, The Andersons, Carolyn Mogey, Louis Freeman, Faulda Rimel and Ron Molito for sharing your knowledge and guidance with me, and for listening to me through the years. Thank you to my dear friends Alex Cousins, Perrin Randlette, Liz Luxenberg, Emily Crabtree, Nha-Vinh Tran, Becca Lawrence, Emma Traore, Marshall and Vera Sonnenberg, Charmaine Constantino, Suzannah Holsenbeck, and Fiach Molloy for spending time with me across this globe, for laughing with me and always inspiring me to live out my dreams.

I would also like to thank Pico Iyer, Carol Canter, Rick Steves, Wild Writing Women, and Bay Area Travel Writers and the many forward thinking writers and travelers who have brought the world closer to me.

Thank you to my incomparable mother and utopia driven father and the rest of my family, blood related and not.

Thank You Khempo.

Introduction

The GrassRoutes Story

Like cracking open a dusty geode, travel has revealed to me the many facets of the world. The crystals I found brought me the clarity to compare my known world with that of the previously unexplored. I was able to truly connect with the rich diversity that abounds. No other activity has had quite the same impact, offering a unique experience where both commonalities and differences in the quilt of humanity were vibrantly displayed. These inspirations occurred while traveling around the globe and around the corner. The cities I have called home have given me plenty of refreshing surprises. Whether boarding a plane for another continent, or walking a few blocks to a nearby neighborhood, no matter what my pocketbook dictated, I always managed to find new cultural gems.

As I walked the gangway on each return flight, I noticed that culture shock was as potent going home as when I had discovered new countries and traditions. Each time my reality was challenged with new ways of thinking and acting, I found I was less attached to one specific culture. After each journey I found I had new interests, different ways of dealing with difficult situations, and an altogether new perspective. The most important souvenir I brought home wasn't tangible—it was a more open mind.

As the pages of my passport filled up with stamps, I had a greater insight into each culture that could never have come from pictures or words. I also had plenty of stories to share. A minor bike accident I incurred in a Kyoto suburb brought a fleet of firemen to my rescue. A similar situation in Denmark roused little notice by other biking commuters, but meant a gratis cup of black coffee as I waited for the city bike to be repaired. (Copenhagen is equipped with its own fleet of public bikes for anyone and everyone's use.) In London, a city stigmatized by many Americans as having the worst food, I have enjoyed some of the finest international cuisines. The more I traveled, the more stereotypes were turned on their head. In short, travel has taught me that no generalization really holds up.

I became a detective of sorts, unearthing cultures. Out of earshot from town squares or famous landmarks, I became familiar with local traditions. When I returned home I kept up the habit, discovering a wealth of intrigue in my own country. As a cultural tourist I discovered unique adventures right around the block. I have since made it my mission to seek out the non-traditional attractions and cities.

The people who hovered around the cathedrals and museums were of greater interest to me than the cold monuments. The living, breathing collection of foods and voices, footsteps on the roads and walkways—those were the things that attracted me. I witnessed the world around me blinking like a disco ball, with authenticity being overtaken by all things virtual, but I trusted in another kind of travel. Wherever I was, the locals gave me the chance to have unique experiences rather than manufactured ones. By focusing on human interaction, serendipity soon replaced artificial stimulation.

GrassRoutes Travel was born out of my growing collection of ideas, inspirations and frustrations. I remembered the grim fact that Americans (United Statesians, actually) have the fewest passports per capita. I made up my mind to promote world citizenship, but search as I might I found no vehicle that expressed my ideas about travel. The Dalai Lama's wise words turned like a prayer wheel in my head: "If you have some [distress] you should examine whether there is anything you can do about it. If you can, there is no need to worry; if you cannot do anything, then there is also no need to worry." Doing something about it turned into GrassRoutes Travel.

The concept evolved from a bundle of notes collected on the road. Since I had never seen cities as separate boroughs, but as one entity, I didn't want my guides to divide chapters by neighborhoods. Most cities aren't so expansive that they warrant being divided by neighborhood. Also, chowing down on some messy barbeque didn't equate with a meal of braised rabbit, so I chose not to organize the guides simply by activity. I thought of the times I had woken up really early, the times I wanted to have a casual night out, or when I needed to get my creative juices flowing. GrassRoutes Travel had to be designed around these states of being: the mood of the traveler(s) and the timing. To find a smash hit burrito at 1 a.m., just turn to the **Up Late** chapter.

But organization wasn't the only thing I wanted to do differently. GrassRoutes Travel is true to its name by including local businesses and their corresponding contributions to the greater good of the community. Restaurants that serve sustainably grown produce share the pages with shops that showcase works by local artists. Wildlife preserves are in the mix with co-operative bakeries and amusements that use energy saving techniques. Some of the best travel experiences I have had have been through meeting the locals in volunteer situations, so an entire chapter focuses on easy ways for visitors and residents alike to interact while giving back. Being conscientious about society and environment is a recipe for peace. Greet the world with an open mind: This is a message I hope to convey.

I was not born with a silver spoon in my mouth. Any voyage I dreamed of had to be financed by yours truly. What I found out was that travel could fit a limited budget. For a quick and cheap adventure, I could check out a new area of town or head to a museum on a free day. (I have included a **City for Free** chapter that lists some great money-free adventures). With a little perseverance, library time and an inquisitive nature, I managed to find work exchange programs, scholarships, cheap fares and home-stays. It was possible, even on my tight budget, to vacation on Mediterranean beaches for a weekend trip while living in Germany, explore the cobblestone walkways of Manchester, UK, and enter a floating temple on the Japanese island of Miyajima. There are ways to afford all kinds of travel. GrassRoutes is more than a guide to a city's attractions, it is a reaffirmation that authentic cultural experiences are not out of reach for anyone.

My first secret is printed right to the cover of this book: visit the city next door. Save time and money by choosing idyllic Rovinj, Croatia instead of over-priced and over-crowded Corfu, Greece for that above-mentioned Mediterranean vacançe. Not only are the next-door cities more affordable, but also they bring you closer to the region because they aren't built up as an attraction in and of themselves. Following the same example, in Rovinj, the native cuisine is delicious. Smoky, delicate fish straight from the surrounding waters with handmade lavender goat cheese just doesn't compare to the toast, eggs and canned beans served at Corfu hostels to keep the many tourists "comfortable".

Along with the sights and sounds, local foods are a window into the uniqueness of each place. By focusing on culinary specialties, GrassRoutes encourages travelers to venture outside their comfort zone.

As you enjoy your travels, you can be satisfied knowing that you are a conscientious consumer. Chocolate cake, conscientious, you ask? You bought it from an organic, co-operative local bakery that supports school gardening programs and purchases sustainably grown ingredients from nearby farms. When I found out how much fun, and, ok, indulgence, could be had while having a positive impact, I chose to be a conscientious consumer. The undeniable facts amassing about the current state of our planet necessitates that more of us make this choice. And with such a bounty of local businesses dedicated to this spirit of positive change, it is becoming easier to support such a philosophy. Each listing in GrassRoutes Travel meets these standards in one aspect or another. So while you are venturing out into the world, and meeting real people in new places, your dollars are staying in the community, supporting everything from waste reduction to entrepreneurial youth, organic food to zero emissions public transit. Becoming a conscientious consumer gives each individual the power to effect positive change in the world.

I bring you GrassRoutes Travel Guides, created to benefit readers and communities. I hope you will try something new, even if you thought it was not possible. Having a genuine cultural escapade is directly proportional to your ability to let go of preconceived notions. All you need is an inquiring mind, a detective's spirit and the desire to get acquainted with the world around you.

Using GrassRoutes Travel Guides

GrassRoutes Travel Guides employ a totally new system of organization that makes searching for activities, restaurants, and venues easy. This guide is organized by situation, with chapters like **Stay Up Late**, **Do Lunch**, and **Hang Out** that pay more attention to your state of being than any other guide.

Organization by type of venue runs the risk of muddling a six-course meal with a drive-thru, just because both are technically restaurants. Instead, shouldn't guides be organized by what kind of dining experience you are looking for, rather than just that you are hungry?

There is a price range key and also a "who to go with" key to highlight great spots to go with friends, solo, with family, or for a romantic time.

All phone numbers are in the **(510)** area code unless otherwise stated.

Price Key:

$- Cheap. Admission costs and entrée prices are under 10 dollars.
$$- Moderate. Entrees between 10 and 15 dollars.
$$$- Pricey. Entrees are over 15 dollars, most are around 20.

Company Key:

S- Solo. These are places and activities that are great experienced alone.
Fr- Friends. Go with one buddy or a group of friends.
Ro- Romance. Great spots to go with that special somebody.
Fam- Family. Places for the whole family to enjoy.
PW- People Watching. These locations are privy to an outpouring of interesting people. Slow down and take in the atmosphere.

Service and Practicality Key:

WiFi- Wireless Internet available free of charge.
R- Reservations recommended
Vn- Vegan entrees available.
Vtn- Vegetarian entrees available.

Travel Tips

There are many different kinds of trips: seeing the seven wonders of the world; doing a trek or outdoor-focused voyage; going to a new city; traveling for family or business that may not involve choosing your own destination; rediscovering your own city when a friend comes to visit. For any given trip there are different ways to plan, but the core remains the same: stay open-minded. I like to remind myself that security is really a false pretense, under which humans can never truly live. This is not to say you should throw yourself to the mercy of the world. Safe travel is smart travel, but judgmental, pre-conceived notion travel can be just as dangerous. I have loads of examples I will spare you with, but suffice it to say, there is a lot out there, and your state of mind is directly relative to how much of the world you will be a part of.

Here are a few tidbits on packing, getting around, trip planning and safety I have compiled over my years of world travel.

Trip Planning

My philosophy for trip planning could be considered a tad unorthodox, but let me just say, it has gotten me far. The bottom line is I don't over plan. I pick dates that make sense, and make the fewest reservations I can get away with. It is crucial to take into consideration factors of time, exhaustion and exploration. Before embarking on a trip, I tell as many people as will listen where I am going and get their feedback and tips. I have the same talkative approach when I am there, meeting locals and finding out their favorite spots. I use guidebooks primarily before the trip and maps during.

Time Allotment

When picking dates, consider what kind of trip you want to have. There is one game plan that spreads out your time between different sights, and serves as a good introduction to an area. Another is spending prolonged time in one or two cities, and getting beneath the skin.

In my experience it is good to slow down the tempo of travel enough to smell the proverbial roses.

Reservations

There are a few practical reasons to make reservations and there are also things I avoid planning too much in advance.

Be sure to reserve a hotel for at least the first night so you have somewhere to go when you get off the plane. Thumbs up to adventure, but even if you travel on a whim I recommend starting on day two after you get your bearings.

If your entire vacation will be spent in the same area, I suggest staying in the same, centrally located hotel the whole time, so you avoid carrying your stuff around. After all, you probably didn't travel to see different hotels, but to see the city itself!

In general, and this depends on the city and country, I wouldn't reserve too many transit engagements. That way if you want to extend your stay in a given spot, you can do that without too many trials and tribulations. Local transit arrangements are usually easy to book without much advance notice. Also, many restaurants don't require, or even accept reservations. That way you can look around, act on a whim and best of all, get the locals' advice. It is hard to get a good sense of a restaurant from their website.

With regards to hotels, make sure you are aware of each place's cancellation policy. Try to get an idea of the city first, before you book a room, so you can place yourself in the area of town that most interests you. (That is why **Lodge** is the located towards the end of this book.) Be sure to reserve special event tickets, and also tables at restaurants that require them. These are noted with an R in this book; see the key in *Using GrassRoutes Travel Guides.*

Packing

I like to have a good pair of pants that can match with different shirts. I would bring one dressier outfit and a bathing suit. Bring more than enough underwear, but wear outfits that can keep their shape for two or three days of use, especially the pants or skirts. You'll be meeting and interacting with new people everyday, so no one will know you wore the same outfit two days in a row. Buy extraneous items like disposable cameras and flip-flops there. Remember, you will have to carry what you bring, so don't weigh yourself down. Check the climate and current weather conditions of your planned locations and pack accordingly.

Safety

Major cities around the world must contend with crime. Please use your wits and stay safe. Try to avoid traveling alone to new places at night.

Other Tips

I always travel with the equipment that makes things less apt to bother me. On the plane I have earplugs and headphones, a sleep mask, a good book and several bottles of water (provided liquid is allowed given new safety regulations). That way even if there is a screaming baby, my voyage will remain blissfully quiet. I find it is easier to make changes yourself than ask others to tone it down.

Get enough sleep before you fly. I would recommend drinking lots of water the day before traveling and the day of, more if you tend to get dehydrated easily or are prone to get headaches from the dry plane air like I am.

Don't plan two activity-heavy days back to back. In general, it is good to have a combination of restful, educational, physical, etc. experiences. That is one of the reasons for the GrassRoutes Guides organization. Traveling can include every type of adventure. The rest of the world gets more vacation time than those in the United States, so Americans risk overdoing it when they actually get time off. The rest of your life is full of work and planning, why make your vacation that way too? Ask yourself what you really want to see and cut out the rest. Keep in mind that you can always come back, and be realistic about what you and your friends and family have the energy for.

I would also recommend breaking into smaller groups when people have different ideas of what they want to see and do. One of my greatest memories was a family vacation where my father and I hiked beside a waterfall together, while my mother relaxed and read at the base of the falls. We were each doing what we wanted, my dad and I got to bond and wave to mom when we got to the top. Notations described in the **Key** indicate which activities are especially good for family, friends, going solo and going for a touch of romance.

Contact Me!

The places and events listed in this guide are ones I thought were outstanding. But cities are constantly changing so please contact me if you feel there is something I missed or you find out-of-date information. Updates, new venues, and corrections will be posted on our website. In any case, I'd love to hear your thoughts and ideas!

info@grassroutestravel.com

www.grassroutestravel.com

About Oakland

The Oak Tree in Frank H. Ogawa Plaza

History

Oakland, California has a rich history marked by innovations and the most ethnically diverse population in the country, with at least 100 languages and dialects spoken. The indigenous people of this land, the Ohlone, invited neighboring tribes to share in the festivities of the bountiful acorn harvest. Today, this spirit is kept alive in Oakland's plethora of cultural celebrations; the city is dedicated to welcoming people of all faiths, races, nationalities and sexualities.

Formerly known as Contra Costa or the "other coast", Oakland reached its status as an incorporated city in 1852. The fledgling city did not go unrecognized, as the Central Pacific Railroad eventually selected Oakland to be the terminus of the transcontinental railroad. The Alameda County seat was relocated to Oakland in 1873.

In 1903, Oakland erected its first skyscraper, an 11-story steel-frame Beaux Arts-style office building at Broadway and 13th Street that houses the Union Savings Bank today. President William H. Taft visited Oakland in 1911 to lay the cornerstone for an even higher City Hall, the first government building designed as a skyscraper and the tallest building west of the Mississippi at the time of its completion.

In the first decade of the 20th Century, Oakland's population more than doubled from 66,960 to over 150,000 as people and businesses relocated from an earthquake-ravaged San Francisco. Oakland was a suitable haven for the victims of the 1906 disaster, especially with the annexation of Claremont, Fruitvale, Elmhurst and other outlying communities in 1909. The city continued to grow, spending over $2 million on the construction of factory buildings in 1918. Less than a decade later, the municipal harbor entered a new era of development as the Port of Oakland. Under the port authority is the 700-acre Oakland Municipal Airport, recognized for launching the first successful flight to Hawaii from the continental US.

The Great Depression and the Second World War brought new growth to the city of Oakland. The population spiked as citizens flocked to Oakland in support of the war effort. During this time, Oakland produced 35% of the entire West Coast cargo ship output. Food packaging became a major industry with 60% of total foodstuffs coming from Oakland canneries.

As Oakland industry grew, the city maintained a strong commitment to preserving natural habitats in the midst of its urban expansion. In 1934, the East Bay Regional Park District grew from 10,000 acres to 50,000 in Alameda County and 42,000 in adjacent Contra Costa County. The district now includes 59 regional parks and a comprehensive network of 29 inter-park trails.

1962 marked the beginning of another period of growth for the city with the arrival of the first container ships. Just two years later, the Port constructed the Seventh Street Marine Terminal, the largest single container terminal on the West Coast. That same year, work began on the award-winning Bay Area Rapid Transit (BART) system. BART began servicing the Bay Area in 1972, with its center of operations located above the Lake Merritt Station in Oakland. The new City Center was completed with the help of matching grants tied to the BART construction project.

Oakland's development plans did not overlook the many historical sites that remained; Preservation Park was conceived to maintain 16 Victorian-era homes. This urban park was developed to resemble a typical 19th century residential Oakland neighborhood. In 1987, Lake Merritt's Necklace of Lights was restored to its 1925 splendor. In 1995, Franklin D. Roosevelt's beloved Floating White House, the USS Potomac, was opened for dockside tours and Bay cruises following a 12-year, $5 million restoration.

On October 17, 1989 the third most lethal earthquake in recorded US history shook the Bay Area. The damage was extensive and included a large expanse of the Cypress Freeway I-880 and a section of the San Francisco-Oakland Bay Bridge. Fortunately, highway traffic was unusually light as many people had left work early to watch Game Three of the World Series, coincidentally between the Oakland A's and the San Francisco Giants. In the following years, Oakland buildings and highways received much-needed seismic retrofits, including Oakland's historic City Hall.

In the 1990s, the National Civic League designated Oakland as an "All-American City" and *Money* magazine ranked Oakland among the top 25 cities to live in the U.S.

Today, Oakland is the seventh largest city in California and among the top 50 in the country. According to the 2000 Census, Oakland ranks 8th in the U.S. in overall educational achievement with more than one-third of the population having earned a college degree. The *Wall Street Journal* named Oakland the number one office market in the country from 2000 through 2005. *Forbes* magazine listed Oakland in the Top 10 for Best Places for Business in 2001 and 2002.

In addition to its rich history, Oakland is the proud home of many innovations and movements, most notably those pertaining to the environment. The Port of Oakland has been committed to conducting its operations in the most sustainable manner possible. Clean water and air programs and habitat restoration developments are top priorities for this thriving container port.

Oakland is also the home of many firsts. C.L. Dellums helped establish the first African American trade union in U.S. history in

1925. In 1983, Robert C. Maynard acquired the Oakland Tribune, making it the first major metropolitan newspaper to be owned by an African American. Mills College was the first all-woman's college in the West, and the first to award a B.A. degree to women west of the Mississippi.

The Center for Women's Business Research ranks Oakland third in the country for the number of women-owned businesses. Many women pioneers have left their mark on Oakland; architect Julia Morgan designed the Webster Street YWCA, one of her major works; Amelia Earhart launched her famous attempted flight around the world from the Oakland Airport; and author Gertrude Stein uttered the most famous quote about Oakland, "there's no there there," (she was actually referring her childhood home when she discovered it had been demolished). In 1997, Linda Finch paid tribute to Earhart by recreating her around-the-world flight in a restored Lockheed Electra 10E aircraft, touching down at Oakland Airport's historic North Field.

Inspiration abounds in Oakland, in its many cultural centers, art collectives and regional parks. In 1886, distinguished poet Joaquin Miller purchased 70 acres in the Oakland Hills and planted 75,000 trees to create an artists' retreat, now Redwood Regional Park. Children's Fairyland, built in 1950, brings children's literature to life and is home to the oldest continuously operating professional puppet theater in the country. The park has also been an inspiration to adults; Walt Disney visited the park while conceiving plans for Disneyland. The internationally acclaimed Oakland Museum, with its tiered Babylonian style roof gardens is devoted to the natural sciences, history and art of California. Heinold's First and Last Chance Saloon, in continuous operation since 1883, was a favorite haunt of writer Jack London, who references the bar 17 times in his novel John Barleycorn.

Oakland is committed to restoring and preserving its historic landmarks. Nearly 130 structures have been declared city landmarks and six areas named preservation districts. The Downtown Oakland Historic District, comprising six city blocks, is listed on the National Register of Historic Places for its architectural significance. Preservation Park won the 1991 Gold Nugget Award as the best restoration project in the West. The Paramount Theatre received an authentic restoration in

1973 to reopen in its original Art Deco splendor. Community organizers are currently raising funds to restore Telegraph Avenue's Fox Theater.

Education has always been at the forefront of Oakland's agenda. The College School, established in 1853, later became the University of California, and the UC Office of the President is located in Downtown Oakland. In 1871, Oakland, ignoring influences from the eastern states, maintained admissions in its public schools for black students. The California College of Arts and Crafts, founded in 1907 by Frederick Meyer, was relocated to Oakland in 1922 and is currently the largest independent art school on the West Coast and the fourth largest in the nation.

Many prominent businesses have their roots in Oakland. Mother's Cookies, the largest cookie producer in the U.S., had its humble beginnings in Oakland, where its headquarters have remained since N.M. Wheatley created the company in 1914. Granny Goose, a large producer of potato chips and crackers started in Oakland in 1946. Victor J. Bergeron founded the successful Trader Vic's Restaurant in Oakland.

Oakland is proud to be the only California city with three professional sports teams: the Oakland Raiders, the Oakland Athletics and the Golden State Warriors. The Raiders began play in 1960 as the eighth charter member of the upstart American Football League and have won three Super Bowls and one AFL Championship. The Oakland A's have won four World Series since relocating from Kansas City in 1968, including three consecutive wins in the 1970s. Oakland native and former A's pitcher Dennis Eckersley was inducted into the Major League Baseball Hall of Fame and is the first of only two MLB pitchers to have a 20-win season and a 50-save season in a career.

Oakland celebrates its diversity in many ways while paying tribute to the welcoming spirit of its original inhabitants. Oakland residents are proud of their city's rich history and strive to preserve its cultural and historical landmarks. The variety of habitats in the Bay Area is remarkable and Oakland is dedicated to sustaining its natural splendor. Countless efforts are made to restore and protect these precious environments so that Oakland will remain a beautiful place for generations to come.

Climate

The National Oceanic and Atmospheric Administration and Rand McNally ranked Oakland's climate the best in the nation. The climate in Oakland is very similar to the Mediterranean. September is the warmest month and January the coldest. Summer weather, mid 70's to 80's, is usually from early June through September. Winter weather is mid 40's to mid 50's, cooler at night as the fog rolls in. The rainy season lasts from November to April with the spring months seeing the most rain. Check out the current weather conditions online before your trip.

Geographically, Oakland is located at 37°48' North, 122°15' West and has a total land area of 56.1 square miles (145.2 kilometers square).

Maps

The following are maps of the major areas of Oakland to help you get around.

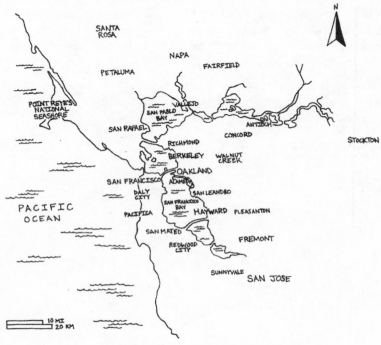

The San Francisco Bay Area

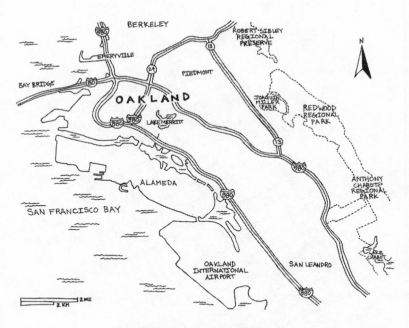

The East Bay and Oakland

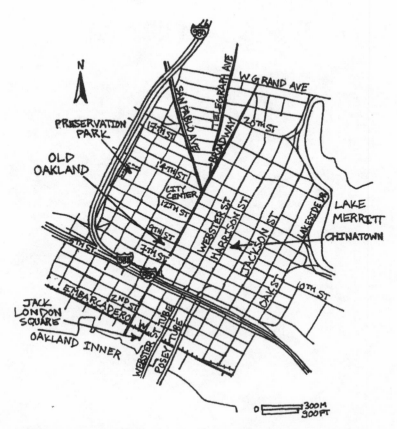

Downtown, Chinatown and Jack London Square.

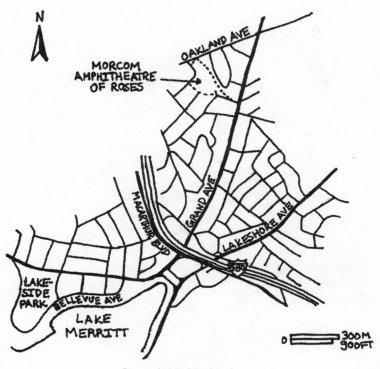

Grand and Lakeshore

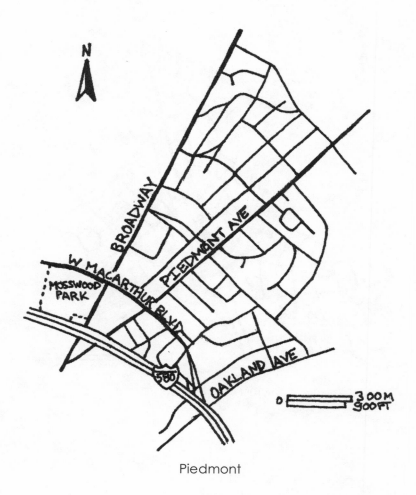

Piedmont

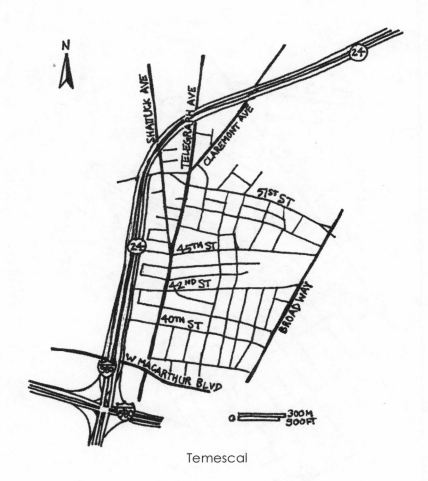

Temescal

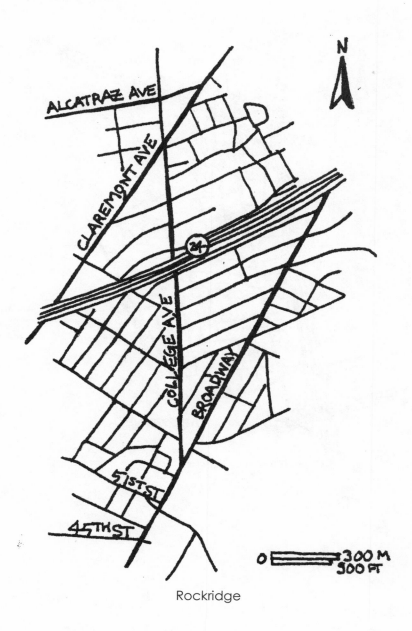

Rockridge

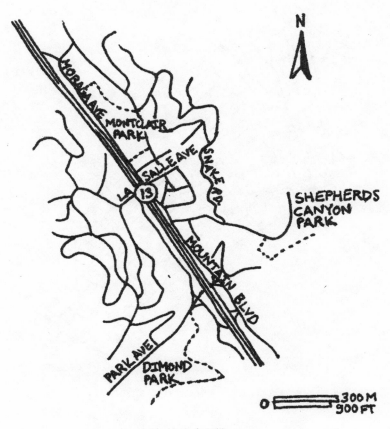

Montclair Village

Dimond and Laurel Districts

Fruitvale

Transit Information

The kind of trip you want to have relates in large part to your mode of travel. It can be convenient to rent a car, but high gas prices, parking fees and traffic can also make it a hassle. Waiting for the bus can try your patience, but it is a cheaper way to go, plus it gives you the opportunity to look around. Biking is a great way to get around until you get to the hills, unless you are a road biker and steep routes are what you are looking for. Safety is also a factor when biking as bike lanes are few and far between in Oakland. Public transportation options offer daily and monthly passes.

Getting Here

The Bay Area is an international travel destination, with three international airports and other major transportation depots. Here's the vital info to get you to Oakland.

Fly Oakland

www.flyoakland.com

Oakland International Airport is a less-crowded, often cheaper alternative to flying into San Francisco. When the weather is bad and the clouds cancel flights to SFO, Oakland remains open and dependable. JetBlue and Southwest are the major carriers. Private shuttles carry passengers to their hotels and final destinations for around 10 dollars. Shuttles connect the airport with the Oakland Coliseum BART station.

Nearby Airports

San Francisco International (SFO) was also recently connected to BART, making it more convenient than San Jose (SJC) for getting to Oakland. Caltrains (www.caltrain.org) also run between these airports, and arrive at Jack London Square and Amtrak's station near Oakland Coliseum (to the southeast of the city).

Train

www.amtrak.com
www.caltrain.org
Caltrain Information Line: 800.660.4287
Amtrak Information Line: 800.USA.RAIL

The major Bay Area terminus for nationwide, long distance train service is Emeryville, only a few blocks away from the Oakland border. Amtrak and Caltrain offer trains from around the Bay Area, and the country, including express service from Sacramento (www.amtrakcapitols.com), Los Angeles, Seattle and Vancouver, Canada. The Zephyr, a rapid train from Chicago, Illinois, also terminates at Emeryville.

Emery-Go-Round

www.emerygoround.com

The Emery-go-Round is a local, free Emeryville bus service that makes it easy for train passengers to get to hotels, and nearby BART and bus stations. Emery-go-Round will pick you up directly from the train station, and go as far as Oakland Coliseum and Oakland International Airport.

AC Transit

www.actransit.org

AC Transit bus routes cover the East Bay and Transbay routes from San Francisco. Selected routes provide over night service; these buses are identified by the addition of 800 to the normal route numbers. Take AC Transit between Amtrak and the Oakland International Airport, or BART stations. Ask the train conductor before disembarking for a Transit Transfer and this service will be free of charge.

Driving

From San Francisco, take Highway 80 east over the Bay Bridge. The western portion of this bridge is as beautiful as the Golden Gate, but often gets over-looked by its famous neighbor. Once you reach the East Bay, choose to go eastward on 580, southwest on 880, or to downtown Oakland by taking the 980.

From points north, take US-101 to 580 and cross the Richmond Bridge, stay on 580, which goes directly into Oakland.

From the Central Coast, take US-101 to San Jose and connect to 880.

From the Central Valley take scenic 580 over the Altamont Pass.

From Contra Costa County, take Highway 24 through the Caldicott Tunnel.

From northern East Bay, and Sacramento follow Interstate 80 into Oakland.

The MacArthur Maze, a scribble of highway interchanges is especially confusing to first time visitors. Highways 980, 24, 880, 580, and 80 join in a tangle, and it doesn't help that they almost all have 80 in them. Have a good look at the map before hand, or enlist a buddy to be your navigator. Worse come to worse, you can get off the highway, re-enter and try again. Sometimes getting lost can bring you closer to a city. (Neldam's Bakery is nestled right below the maze, so you can award yourself with a cookie or muffin as prize for missing your exit).

Greyhound Bus
www.greyhound.com

The Greyhound station is on San Pablo Avenue at 20th Street, just north of Old Oakland.

Getting Around

Here is all the information you need to plan your trips around Oakland.

Transit Information
www.transitinfo.org

All relevant Bay Area transit information is on this website. On a local phone, dial 511 for exact schedules and routes for any destination in the Bay, including carpooling information. 511 makes it extremely easy for anyone to use a combination of Bay Area public transit systems Current traffic conditions on Bay Area highways is also available.

BART (Bay Area Rapid Transit)
www.bart.gov

BART is the award-winning rapid transit system serving the East Bay, Peninsula, and San Francisco. There are many stops in Oakland, including a convenient air-shuttle connection to the Oakland International Airport. BART cards, available from vending machines in each station, can be purchased in any amount for a single trip or multiple trips; fare charts are posted. You can carry your bike on BART providing it isn't during rush hour (7:05-8:50am and 4:25-6:45pm). BART-to-bus transfer discounts are available from the white machines, remember to pick one up before you leave the paid area of the station if you plan on connecting to AC Transit.

Ferry
www.eastbayferry.com

The Alameda-Oakland Ferry sails between Pier 41 and the Ferry Building in San Francisco to Alameda and Jack London Square in Oakland. Transit time from San Francisco is about 30 minutes. Ferries operate seven days a week with more boats departing during commuter hours in the morning and evening. The last ferry arrives in Oakland around 11pm. During baseball season, ferries sail directly to the stadium in San Francisco. Check the website for up-to-date schedules and fares.

During the summer you can catch a ferry from Oakland to Angel Island, which I highly recommend. Angel Island is a beautiful park, with stunning views of the entire bay. It has been transformed from its dark past as an unscrupulous immigration station. Ferries are a wonderful way to get out on the water and see the greater Bay Area.

AC Transit
www.actransit.org

AC Transit is the East Bay's primary bus system. Buses require exact change for the $1.75 fare, and charge an extra $.25 for transfers. The website is the best place to find exact routes and up-to-date fares. Call 511 for last minute info, or traffic reports that effect bus routes. A transfer is good for one additional bus ride in any direction, including a return trip, but must be used within 3 hours of the original ride. Buses numbered in the 800's are night-owl routes.

Serena's Top Picks

Of all the sights and delights around Oakland, these are my absolute favorites.

Lake Merritt Stroll

A leisurely stroll around Lake Merritt, whether with the early crowd, or at twilight when the hanging lights are aglow, is a relaxing way to see the heart of the city. Check out the country's first wildlife preserve and a grand collection of bonsai along the northern rim of the lake.

Wednesday Night A's Games

Baseball began as a game for the people, a national pastime. Unfortunately many stadiums today charge high prices for tickets, making the sport inaccessible for some. The Oakland Athletics have maintained a large enough stadium to offer cheap seats, and every Wednesday, tickets for the upper level are only two dollars. It is a day when many people share this authentic American experience.

Flint's Bar-B-Q

Flint's serves the best barbeque in the East Bay. 'Nuff said.

Oakland Symphony Orchestra

One of the best orchestra's in the country is right here in Oakland. Often living in the shadow of other more well-known ensembles, these talented musicians are top notch.

Tourettes Without Regrets

This rowdy Thursday night show represents the wealth of up and coming talents in the Bay Area. Poets, emcees and freestylers gather to put on a lively performance. The first Thursday of each month at The Oakland Metro (see **Listen** chapter) you will find a huge line forming just before 8pm. This is a loud event, and uses words and beats as a mode of release, including cursing and non-PC material.

Oliveto

Oliveto is an amazing restaurant, where each menu item stands out. No matter what you order, your taste buds will be on cloud nine. It is the best place for celebrating the accomplishments of your friends and family—in fact there's no place I'd rather go for my birthday (hint, hint).

Redwood Park Hiking and Concerts

The groves of redwoods that cover the hilltops of Oakland are a world away from the urban downtown. Hug a tree the size of a car, and then hike up and down through a maze of ferns and pine needles. Summer and Fall concert series take place each year, featuring many local groups. This park is unlike any other existing inside a city's boundaries.

Grand Lake Theater

The Grand Lake Theater lives up to the real magic of the movies. With the Wurlitzer organ welcoming you, and Tiffany glass displays to enjoy, this theater is an Oakland gem.

World Cup Coffee Tamales

The Tamale Queen fires up her grill every morning to hand roast the scrumptious ingredients for her corn treats. The back patio of this coffee shop is home to the finest Tamales around, a filling and inexpensive treat.

Chabot Telescope Viewings

Friday and Saturday nights, Chabot's world-famous telescope is open to the public for planetary viewings. As long as the sky is clear enough, you can come up the hill and take a peak at a current highlight of the night sky. There is no better way to see the stars than through this lens, one of the most powerful telescopes in the country. Astronomers are on-site to answer questions and explain exactly what you are seeing.

Old Oakland Farmers Market

There is truly nothing like Old Oakland's Friday morning Farmer's Market. Afghani spices, Southern jambalayas, Vietnamese greens and organic, locally grown berries fill the abundant stands near historic Swan's Market. The richness of Oakland's diverse community joins together as a treat for any taste buds. Live music and craft stalls are also in the mix.

For International Visitors

Required Documents

Contact the nearest U.S. Embassy or Consulate for visa, passport, and health requirements.

Customs

You must complete customs and immigrations formalities at your first point of arrival in the U.S., whether or not it is your final destination.

Travel Insurance

The U.S. has no compulsory government plan. It is advisable to purchase private travel and health insurance.

Foreign Language Assistance

Call 1.888 US-1-INFO (1.888.871.4636) for free access to emergency services and travel assistance in more than 140 languages.

Electricity

The standard electrical current is 110 volts. Most outlets accept two or three pronged plugs. Laptops and other electronic devices should be equipped with a power converter.

Currency

Most large banks and several independent bureaus exchange major foreign currencies. The San Francisco and San Jose Airports have exchange offices in their international terminals. Traveler's checks in U.S. dollars and credits cards are widely accepted.

The following lists local exchange bureaus:

Northern California Coin Exchange
3356 Grand Avenue at Lake Park Avenue

Lucky Money
1753 Broadway at 17th Street

Emergencies

Oakland is an international city, equipped with modern emergency facilities and service in Spanish, Cantonese and English. As part of the *Corridor of Safety* Oakland is the center of a hi-tech alert and warning system in the event of a major disaster. Because this city has experienced earthquakes and fires in the past, the emergency departments are especially experienced and well prepared. Oakland has a number of citywide safety programs to educate the community. Its businesses ensure that they are outfitted with the appropriate emergency kits.

Warning System

In the event that the city warning sirens sound, follow three simple steps: Shelter, Shut and Listen. (See the Alameda County website for more information, or to attend a safety training course free of charge: www.acgov.org.)

Emergency Broadcasts

Oakland designates 530AM for emergency radio broadcasts.

KTOP Channel 10 is the city's public television network where emergency information will also be available.

The city website is www.oaklandnet.com

Emergency Contacts

Foreign language lines, for emergency information translated to Spanish and Cantonese primarily (French and Mandarin are also available, but information is from San Leandro, the town south of Oakland) 510.444.CITY and 510.618.1610

If you are in an emergency, dial 911 from any home, business, or pay phone.

The **Oakland Police Department** should be dialed directly if using a cellular telephone: 510.777.3211

Oakland Police non-emergency number: 510.777.3333

For immediate, non-emergency medical care, the Ambulatory Health Care Services Administration operates several clinics in Highland Hospital where visitors can be seen by doctors and specialists. Confidential HIV and pregnancy testing are also available.

Highland Hospital
Primary and Specialist Clinics
1411 East 31st Street at 14th Avenue Oakland
Main Number: 510.437.4800
Appointments: 437.8500

Calendar

Annual cultural events and festivities are part of what make Oakland such an exciting place. Check out what will be going on when you'll be in town and take the opportunity to get involved in one or more of these great activities. There is something for everyone.

Dates vary from year to year, check the Oakland City website for up to date information. Any branch of the Oakland Public Library will have listings of what is going on. The Oakland Tribune and East Bay Express (free) also have some event information, as well as concerts and one-time events.

Resources:
www.oaklandnet.com
www.oaklandlibrary.org

Annual Tribute to Dr. Marin Luther King Jr.- Weekend before MLK Day, January

300 Lakeside Drive at 14th Street
464.7139
www.oaklandnet.com/celebrations

Each year there is a new theme for this multimedia presentation, coupled with hands on activities for the whole family.

Volunteer Day at MLK Shoreline- MLK Day, January

Arrowhead Marsh, Martin Luther King Jr. Regional Shoreline
Swan Way at Doolittle Drive
562.1373
www.ebparks.org

"A day on, not a day off" is the idea behind this citywide community volunteer day.

Expressing the Dream Show- MLK Day, January

Malonga Casquelourd Center for the Arts
1428 Alice Street at 14th Street
238.7217

Every year amazing musicians, poets and performers gather to put on a show as a tribute to the great MLK.

Chinese New Year Festival- Lunar New Year, end of January, beginning of February

Oakland Chinatown
893.8979

Ongoing music, food and festivities take over the heart of Oakland for the ultimate lunar New Year festivities.

Oakland Tet Festival- Lunar New Year

Clinton Square Park
6th Avenue at International Boulevard
612.7071
www.vaced.org

The annual Tet festival is a fun celebration featuring Vietnamese food, activities and entertainment.

Lunar New Year Celebration- Lunar New Year

Oakland Museum of California
1000 Oak Street at 10th Street
238.2200
www.museumca.org

The first day of the lunar New Year goes off with a bang at the Oakland Museum. Check out Taiko drumming, dragon dancers, and acrobats, plus storytelling, arts and crafts and tasty treats for all.

Chinese New Year's Bazaar- beginning of February

Oakland Chinatown
893.8979

All the bounty of Chinese culture comes alive with music, arts, food and great shopping.

African American Celebration through Poetry- February

West Oakland Branch Public Library
1801 Adeline Street at 18th Street
238.7352
www.oaklandlibrary.org

Another great free event is this annual open mic and poetry showcase. Come prepared with a poem and get ready to be inspired!

African American History Month- February
African American Museum and Library
125 14th Street at Martin Luther King Jr. Way
238.4980

An array of different programs and events are scattered around town throughout the entire month.

Annual White Elephant Sale- early March
333 Lancaster Street at Glascock Street
238.2200
www.museumca.org

Planes, trains, or taxis, take whatever mode of transit necessary, but don't miss this world famous sale of everything under the sun. All proceeds go to the Oakland Museum's Women's Board

Jewish Music Festival- mid-March
Berkeley, Oakland and Richmond Jewish Community Centers
848.0237

Performers of all kinds celebrate Jewish tradition with classic and modern tunes everyone can enjoy.

Tall Ship Expo- March
Jack London Square, Broadway at Embarcadero West
800.200.5239

To kick off the sailing season, famous ships dock in the harbor for a fun, up-close look at the wonderful world of big boating.

Annual CPR Preparedness Day- mid-March
Various Locations
Register online
Classes offered in several languages
www.bayarearedcross.org

Free CPR and First Aid classes are offered all day at several locations. Take this opportunity to be a safer citizen.

Easter Egg Hunt- Easter Sunday

Arroyo Viejo Park
7701 Krause Avenue at 77th Avenue
Old Fashioned Easter

Oakland's official egg hunt brings families together for fun, games, music and food. Join council members and city clubs in welcoming the spring.

Easter Sunday

Dunsmuir Historic Estate
2960 Peralta Oaks Court at Peralta Oaks Drive
615.555
www.dunsmuir.org

There is lots of fun to be had with old-time Easter games and the bunny herself. Bring a basket.

Strictly Sail Pacific- mid-April

Jack London Square, Broadway at Embarcadero West
800.817.SAIL (7245)
www.sailamerica.com

The Pacific Sail Expo draws hundreds of exhibitors and sailboats together for the biggest boating fest west of the Mississippi.

Knit and Crochet Show- last weekend in April

Oakland Marriot City Center
1001 Broadway at 10th Street
www.knitandcrochetshow.com
Print admission coupons at the website

Classes, supplies, fashion shows and a silent auction to help fight breast cancer make this a great way to celebrate this age-old hobby.

Earth Day- April 22, or the closest Saturday

Call for staging locations
238.7611

"Clean it. Green it. Mean it." Thousands of volunteers from around the city gather together to restore creeks, plant public gardens, cleanup communities, and enjoy a day of neighborhood beautification.

The Potomac's Opening Day on the Bay- end of April
540 Water Street at Washington Street
627.1215
www.usspotomac.org

The USS Potomac is joined by a fleet of smaller boats for a lunch cruise around the bay Presidential style.

Astronomy Day- beginning of May
Jack London Square, Broadway at Embarcadero West
587.6052
www.jacklondonsquare.com

Celebrate astronomy by viewing sunspots, far-off planets and our very own moon.

Cinco de Mayo Festival and Parade- first Sunday in May
International Boulevard between 33rd and 40th Avenues
536.6084
www.oaklandcincodemayo.com

One of the best family events of the year, this traditional celebration commemorates the victory of the Mexicans over the French in 1862. Entertainment, vendors, food and activities accompany a huge and lively parade.

Mother of the Year- Mother's Day
Morcom Rose Garden
700 Jean Street at Grand Avenue

This annual ceremony is an Oakland tradition, celebrating strong female community activists. It takes place as the roses are reaching full bloom.

Bike to Work Day- mid-May
Frank H. Ogawa Plaza at 14th Street and Broadway
www.oaklandpw.com/bicycling

Bike to Work Day is a statewide event that gets commuters really moving. Come be a part of the huge *Energizer Station* in front of City Hall, win prizes and get involved in the *no-pollute* commute!

Festival of Greece- last weekend in May

Greek Orthodox Church
4700 Lincoln Avenue at Lincoln Way
531.3400
www.asencioncathedral.org

This huge event is a total immersion into the richness of Greek traditions and flavors. Dancing, music, arts and the most delicious food make this one fest that can't be missed.

Step Forward to Cure Tuberous Sclerosis- end of May

Begins at Jack London Square, Broadway at Embarcadero West
483.9958
www.tsalliance.org

This fundraiser provides the chance to enjoy a 1.9-mile circular scenic walkathon and post-walk comedy event where all proceeds go towards improving treatment of this disease.

Family Explorations! Shake It, Don't Break It- end of May

Oakland Museum of California
1000 Oak Street at 10th Street
238.2200
www.museumca.org

Bring the whole family to explore a common California phenomenon: earthquakes. Learn how to get prepared and how earthquakes work. Create a disaster preparedness kit. Build Lego houses and watch them withstand a simulated earthquake.

Himalayan Fair- last weekend in May

Live Oak Park
1301 Shattuck Avenue at Berryman Street, Berkeley
869.3995

The Bay Area's Nepali, Tibetan and Bhutanese communities put on this inspiring event with crafts and ongoing performances. Try regional cuisine while you shop for handmade treasures.

Visuals and Voice Art Exhibit- end of May
Jack London Square, Broadway at Embarcadero West
www.jacklondonsquare.com

This is an annual traveling eco-art, photography and poetry show for high school students exhibiting their environmental art creations.

Carnival- Memorial Day Weekend
Mission Economic Cultural Association
415.826.1401

San Francisco's Carnival is like traveling to South America for the day. This yearly street party and parade is truly epic. Take BART across the bay.

Family Sundays
Weekends throughout the Summer
Dunsmuir Historic Estate
2960 Peralta Oaks Court at Peralta Oak Drive
615.555
www.dunsmuir.org

Mansion tours and picnics are a relaxed way to spend family time and get connected with Oakland's history.

Juneteenth- Father's Day
Adeline Street between Ashby and Alcatraz Avenues
Juneteenth Assn.
655.8008, 654.1461

This is a colorful street fair complete with all the necessities to have a truly memorable Father's Day. There's music, games, stalls and plenty of food.

Walk in the Wild- mid-June
Oakland Zoo, Knowland Park
9777 Golf Links Road off of Interstate 580 exit
632.9525
www.oaklandzoo.org

Enjoy tastings from some of the East Bay's finest wineries, breweries, and restaurants.

Annual Woodminster Cross Country Trail Race- end of June

Joaquin Miller Park
Pinewood Area on Joaquin Miller Road
655.8228

Immerse yourself in nature at it's finest in the beautiful hills of Oakland, while participating in a 9-mile cross-country race. Medals for 1st through 15th place will be awarded with special Woodminster Survivor Awards to the first 250 finishers.

Lesbian, Gay, Bisexual, Transgender Pride Parade- weekend in Late June

Take BART across the Bay
415.864.3733

This amazing San Francisco parade is famous around the world for its creative costumes and acceptance of all people, no matter what their sexual orientation.

Play Day on the Plaza- beginning of July

1 Frank H. Ogawa Plaza at 14th Street
238.PARK

July is National Recreation and Parks Month. The city of Oakland celebrates by hosting events throughout the city.

Alameda County Fair- two weeks in July

Alameda County Fairgrounds
4501 Pleasanton Avenue at Rose Avenue, Pleasanton
925.426.7600

Rides, games, pie contests, and all the trappings of an old-fashioned county fair make summer time complete. Come see the cow contest and the goat showdown in the farm tents.

4th of July Celebration- July 4th

Jack London Square, Broadway at Embarcadero West
866.295.9853
www.jacklondonsquare.com

Oakland's biggest Independence Day celebration is at Jack London Square! Live music performances, festival foods, arts and crafts, and carnival games provide fun for the entire family. An exciting fireworks show will explode over the estuary beginning at 9:15 pm.

Oakland Municipal Band- July 4

Edoff Memorial Bandstand
666 Bellevue Avenue at Grand Avenue

The band plays a traditional lakeside concert to celebrate the fourth.

Annual Scottish Highland Games- first weekend in July

Dunsmuir Historic Estates
2960 Peralta Oaks Court at Peralta Oaks Drive
615.5555
www.dunsmuir.org

Revel in traditional Celtic music, athletic competitions, Scottish country and Irish Step Dancing, clan displays, living history reenactments, children's activities, authentic Scottish foods, craft vendors and more bagpipes and kilts than you can shake a caber at.

Girls Sports Day at Bushrod Field- mid-July

Bushrod Park
560 59th Street at Shattuck Avenue
597.5031

Play all kinds of games with the girls that come to win!

Black Expo- mid-July

Oakland Convention Center
1001 Broadway at 10th Street
839.0690

Job fair, entertainment, music, college expo and much more focus on the African American community.

McCrea Pond Fly-Fishing Demonstrations- mid-July
McCrea Park Pond
4460 Shepherd Street at Carson Street

Check out this classic sport with a first-hand demonstration.

Montclair Fine Arts Sidewalk Festival- end of July
Montclair Business Improvement District
Mountain Boulevard at La Salle Avenue
339.1000

Bay Area artists come together to show off their talents on the streets of Montclair.

Laurel World Music Festival- mid-August
MacArthur Boulevard, between 35th Avenue and 38th Avenue
301.3122
www.laureldistrictassociation.org

Groove to world music, a street fair and kid's activities with international flair.

CircusFit- mid-August
Josie de la Cruz Park
1637 Fruitvale Avenue at East 16th Street

Ringling Bros. clowns lead children and their parents in a community aerobics class and go over the basics of healthy nutrition.

Outdoor Cinema-August and September
Old Oakland
9th Street at Washington Street
238.4734
www.filmoakland.com

Free movies are shown on an outdoor screen in the historic heart of Oakland! Free parking is available at 8th and Washington. Some chairs are provided but bring your own for a guaranteed seat.

Chinatown Streetfest- last weekend in August
9th Street and Franklin Street
893.8979
www.oaklandchinatownstreetfest.com

Sample memorable Asian cuisine and shop for unique gifts. Live entertainment includes Chinese Lion dancing and martial arts demonstrations.

Annual Sistahs Steppin' in Pride- end of August
Snow Park's Sistah Village
Harrison Street between 19th & 20th Streets
534.9603
www.SistahsSteppin.org

Join Sistahs Steppin' in Pride for an afternoon of entertainment, vendors, food, and fun! Bring your friends, your drum (or borrow one), and join up to fill the streets with voices and merrymaking!

Art and Soul Festival- Labor Day weekend
Frank H. Ogawa Plaza at 14th Street
444.2489
www.oaklandculturalarts.org
www.artandsouloakland.org

Experience three sensational days of music, food, fun and art in beautiful downtown Oakland. Live rock, blues, jazz, gospel and more jam on five concert stages. Exciting national and local acts blended with culturally diverse art, poetry, music and food. Children of all ages revel in the Family Fun Zone. There is easy BART access and free parking for thousands of cars

Shoreline Clean-Up- Saturdays in September
Shorebird Nature Center
644.8623

Join East Bay communities for a shore-side cleanup to help restore wildlife populations in this beautiful area.

Sundays in the Redwoods- September and October

Woodminster Amphitheatre
3300 Joaquin Miller Road at Crane Way
238.7275

A free concert series running for four consecutive Sundays beginning in September features the Oakland East Bay Symphony.

Black Filmworks- late September

Black Filmmakers Hall of Fame
410 14th Street at Franklin Street
465.0804
Oakland International Film Festival

This incredible film and video festival features some of the most talented filmmakers who hail from *Oaktown*. Material ranges from hilarious to historical.

Oakland International Film Festival- September

Various Locations
451.FILM
www.oiff.org
www.oaklandfilmfestival.org

This festival showcases international narrative, documentary and animated films at Oakland's Grand Lake Theater.

Annual "A Taste of California"- end of September

Oakland Museum of California
1000 Oak Street at 10th Street
238.2200
www.museumca.org

Dress up or not for this casually elegant event for guests over 21, featuring wine, specialty beers, an array of gourmet food, art, music and a silent auction.

Annual Black Cowboy Parade- first weekend in October

West Oakland & Downtown
655.7309

Celebrate the cowboys who helped settle the West, featuring cowboys from all over the country, trick riders and children dressed in traditional Western attire.

Fleet Week Cruise- first weekend in October

540 Water Street at Washington Street
627.1215
www.usspotomac.org
www.jacklondonsquare.com

The USS Potomac is cruising during Fleet Week, which features the Blue Angels Navy precision flying team.

Indigenous Peoples Day- Saturday closest to October 12th

Various Locations
Indigenous Peoples Committee, Berkeley
595.5520

Witness a traditional Pow Wow and honor the first peoples of this land.

United Nations Parade- end of October

Jack London Square, Broadway at Embarcadero West
866.295.9853
www.jacklondonsquare.com

Celebrate the birthday of the United Nations.

Universoul Circus- a week in late October

5601 Oakport Street at 66th Avenue
800.316.7439
www.universoulcircus.com

View mesmerizing trapeze artist, Shanghai Swingers from the Orient, Caribbean Flava stilt walkers and Limbo Mamas, acts by Ameera Diamond Elephant Trainer, and much, much more!

Moon Viewing Festival- October during the Full Moon

Lake Merritt, off Grand Avenue
981.6166

Relax or stroll around Lake Merritt and view the moon with the community. Participate in lunar activities and music with a lunar theme.

Boo at the Zoo- Last Weekend in October

Oakland Zoo, Knowland Park
9777 Golf Links Road off of Interstate 580 exit
632.9525
www.oaklandzoo.org

Give the animals something to look at by donning a costume for daytime Halloween fun, parade, and more.

Jack O' Lantern Jamboree- End of October

Children's Fairyland
Bellevue Way at Grand Avenue
452.2259
www.fairyland.org

More delightful than frightful, this is a Halloween extravaganza for the little ones.

Annual Haunted Harbor and Boat Parade- End of October

Jack London Square, Broadway at Embarcadero West
800.645.5968
www.jacklondonsquare.com

Have fun decorating Trick or Treat bags with the ProArts artists or be captivated by the Mystery Machine that transforms into a theater for children to watch a Halloween special. Stay till it gets dark and watch a spectacular lighted boat show as scary, haunted water vessels pass through the night carrying the spirits of pirates who were lost at sea.

Dia de Los Muertos- end of October

Fruitvale District, near International Boulevard and Foothill Boulevard
535.6904

Celebrate the dead, at this culturally rich Latino festival. Enjoy music, colorful altars, ethnic foods, arts, crafts, and kids activities.

Annual Tree Lighting Ceremony- Thanksgiving Weekend

Jack London Square, Broadway at Embarcadero West
866.295.9853
www.jacklondonsquare.com

Join the official lighting of the Jack London Square holiday tree. Watch as 20 Bay Area high schools compete in a $5000 choir competition sponsored by the radio station KBLX. Holiday shop for arts and crafts, visit Santa, and get into the holiday spirit with live music. Actual tree lighting will take place at 6pm.

Holidays at Dunsmuir- throughout December

Dunsmuir Historic Estate
2960 Peralta Oaks Court at Peralta Oaks Drive
615.5555
www.dunsmuir.org

Take a tour of the historic mansion and then partake in the a la carte tea service. Entertainment and displays include carolers, horse-drawn carriages for hire, craft booths, and children's activities.

Lighted Yacht Parade- First Weekend in December

Great views from Jack London waterfront, at Embarcadero West

The reflection of thousands of lights on the bay waters is simply mesmerizing.

Up Early

Early bird specials and other morning treats

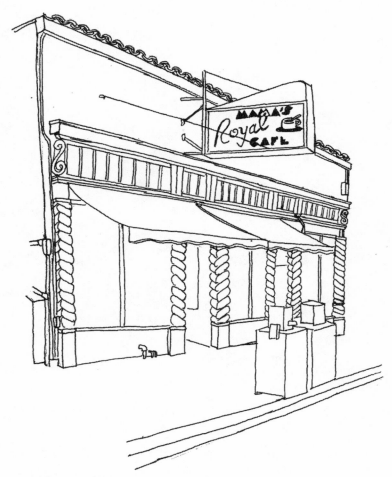

Mama's Royal Café, Broadway

Even on vacation there are times when you wake up with an extra gusto. A morning walk, or a nice long breakfast can help you start a day of exploration off right. Take time to enjoy the simple things, follow your nose on a whim. I like taking it easy, stepping back for a moment from all our electronic systems and just letting my feet go for a stroll. Here are some of my favorite spots to enjoy in the early morning, alone or with a friend.

Mama's Royal Café

4012 Broadway at Ridgeway Avenue
547.7600
Open: M-F 7a-3p, Sat-Sun 8a-3p
$ Fr Fam Vtn

Mama's Royal is one of the staple eateries in Oakland. Back in the 60's it opened with a revolutionary take on diners. Instead of frozen orange juice concentrate they used fresh squeezed, locally grown Valencias. Instead of cheerios, they made their own granola. The crab sandwich isn't made of fake crab, or even canned or frozen crab, but freshly steamed king crab. To this day they offer a local feel to diner classics, and have also added their own innovations to the menu. The Dagwood sandwich is one such item, toppled sky high with turkey, avocado, a fried egg, some bacon, tomato, cheese, and more. Try a tofu scramble, or one of their flavorful omelets, filled with chunks of organic sausage. The funky décor comes with loads of funny stories on which the waitresses would be happy to elaborate. One of the servers hangs his collection of frilly aprons from a wall. This place was put in the **Up Early** chapter for a reason—if you get there too late you'll wait a long time for a table. Bring cash 'cause they don't take plastic.

Temescal Café

4920 Telegraph Avenue at 49th Street
595.4102
Open: M-F 7a-9p, Sat 8a-9p, Sun 9a-9p
$ S Vtn

This local hangout serves a good cup of coffee and a nice pot of tea. Most of the customers are regulars who come to catch up on news and events, or work on a knitting project while munching on quiche or buttermilk waffles with poached eggs. There is a great bulletin board, and evening entertainment as well.

Rockridge Café

5492 College Avenue at Lawton Avenue
653.1567
www.rockridgecafe.com
Open: M-Sat 730a-3p, Sun 8a-3p
$ Fr Fam Vtn Vn

With huge booths and large round tables, this is the best place to go with a bunch of friends for a comforting breakfast. The food is nourishing, the coffee is good and the prices are right. On weekends, families pile in by the boatload to gather around their stellar breakfast classics.

Full House

3719 MacArthur Boulevard at Loma Vista Avenue
482.2200
Open: Tu-Sun 730a-230p
$ Fam Vtn

Other places in Oakland may serve good pancakes, gingerbread pancakes, lemon ricotta pancakes... the list goes on. But what about good old buttermilk? Full House gets my first place vote for their fluffy basic buttermilk pancakes, which soar far above the rest with their air-pocketed texture. Try the red hash (it has beets in it) and the many flavors of coffee cake too. It's packed on the weekends.

Lake Merritt Colonnade, El Embarcadero

Lake Merritt Walking Path

Parking on Bellevue Avenue at Grand Avenue
www.oaklandnet.com/parks/parks/lakemerritt.asp

If you can believe it, Lake Merritt was actually the first official wildlife preserve in the US. It began as a kind of sanctuary where sea birds and land fowl could share common ground. There still remains a small petting zoo, and plenty of birds, which have the unfortunate habit of doing their business everywhere. There is a neat path around the lake that is just the right distance and provides respite from the intensity of city life. I also like to stroll here at sundown when the hanging lights get turned on and the Tribune tower starts to glow. If you are a jogger or dog walker this is the perfect place to start the day.

Old Oakland Farmers Market

9th Street between Broadway and Clay Street
745.7100
www.urbanvillageonline.com/oldoakland
Fridays, all year 'round 8a-2p

Few farmers markets include such a wide variety of international foods. If you get there early, you can buy fresh fish, while listening to live jazz. Vietnamese vegetables are piled next to Afghani spices, next to Chinese greens and free-range eggs. There is a fantastic orchid seller, and also some craft stands which vary from week to week. Bread and baked goods also abound, as well as fresh flower stands. It is right next to Café 817 (see **Do Lunch** chapter), so you can have a nice coffee or nibble after buying fresh produce from around the globe.

Egg Shop

6126 Medau Place at Moraga Avenue
339.3588
Open: M-Sat 10a-3p, Sun 8a-2p
$ Fr Vtn

For the best omelets in town, head to the Egg Shop. Housed in what looks like an old train depot, complete with a circulating electric train. The menu is chock-full of yummy breakfast classics. I like to go when I get that hungry grumble in my belly upon waking up.

Do Lunch

Outstanding mid-day eating of every sort

Café 817, Washington Street

Lunch is my favorite meal of the day. When I lived in Switzerland it was an event, with several courses and mandatory attendance by the entire family. In fact, some parts of the world consider this the largest meal of the day. There are many types of lunches to be had, from sloppy sandwiches to Cambodian salads to Chinese hot pots. The wealth of diversity is evidenced in Oakland's wonderful lunch spots—and even though I have avoided the typical "eat" or "restaurant" chapters of other guidebooks, I feel that lunch is such a state of mind, it had to have a place of it's own.

Caffé 817

817 Washington Street at 8th Street
271.7965
www.cafe817.com
Open: M-F 730a-4p, Sat 830a-3p
$$ PW Vtn

Caffé 817 serves the freshest local ingredients possible, but more importantly it creates the most divine dishes out of them. Salads of perfectly dressed baby maché with seared tuna and eggs go great with a tea blossom (watch it bloom as it steeps). The paninis are fabulous too. The plates are just the right size to fill you up but not overdo it. This is truly one of my favorite places to eat in Oakland. After discovering the lunches I came in for breakfast after a romp at the farmers market. They hit the same mark with their frühstück: the poached eggs with truffle tapenade are out of this world.

Barney's Gourmet Hamburger

4162 Piedmont Avenue at Echo Avenue
655.7180
5819 College Avenue at Chabot Road
601.0444
www.barneyshamburgers.com
Open: Everyday 11a-930p
$ Fr Fam Vtn Vn

No matter how this country gets carried away with diets and low-carb options, the truth is we all want a good burger and fries sometimes, even vegetarians and vegans. And that is where Barney's comes in. One of the few chains in this book, Barney's is still a locally owned and operated business that serves such tasty grub it has spread through many neighborhoods on both sides of the bay. Their four-page menu covers every possible burger topping, served on everything from French baguettes, to multigrain rolls or sesame buns. Traditional beef can be swapped for nitrate-free turkey or three types of vegan bean-based patties. Choose from hand-cut fries, or curly cues. The Turkish coffee shake is unbelievable; even though I try to steer away from shakes, this one is irresistible—make an exception!

Christopher's Burger

5295 College Avenue at Manila Avenue
601.8828
Open: Everyday 1130a-9p
$ Fr S

Christopher's offers a plethora of burger toppings heaping over with fresh ingredients. Try their homemade mayonnaise or aioli; the chipotle goes great on the salmon burger. Service is always friendly and quick, keeping even the hungriest happy.

Mi Grullense Taco Truck

29th Avenue at International Boulevard
Open: Hours vary, open everyday during daylight hours, and into the night on weekends.
$ Fr

Taco Trucks are an important part of the Oakland dining scene and Mi Grullense has the best tacos around. Swing by for a snack anytime. Each taco is served open-faced on a corn tortilla with a wide variety of toppings to choose from. The adventurous diner can sample brain and tongue tacos. I stick with steak, chorizo (Mexican sausage) or carnitas (pulled pork). Vibrant sauces contribute to the messiness of the meal, but for under 2 dollars a taco, who's complaining. Burritos and Tortas (Mexican sandwiches) are also on the menu, but there is a good reason they're called taco trucks, tacos are what they do best.

Holy Land (Kosher)

677 Rand Avenue at Lake Park Avenue
272.0535
Open: Lunch Sun-F, Dinner Sun-Th, Closed Jewish Holidays and Shabbat
$ Fr S Vtn

Shopping makes me thirsty! And since Holy Land makes the best lemonade in the universe, I head to tucked-away Rand Avenue for refreshment. The lemonade is like a lemon slushy, not too sweet, with fresh mint and real lemons. They also have authentic crunchy falafels with creamy hummus for a snack, and outstanding beet salad. Rand is wedged between Lakeshore and Grand Avenues, both great places to browse and explore. If you are winding down from a walk around Lake Merritt, it's a stone's throw from the colonnade, so really there's no excuse for not stopping in.

Bakesale Betty

5098 Telegraph Avenue at 51st Street
985.1213
www.bakesalebetty.com
Open: Tu-Sat 7a-7p
$ Vtn

I was late for work one day and wanted one of Betty's sandwiches to go, but sadly they weren't going to be ready for another 25 minutes. The sweet girl behind the counter handed me a paper bag with a fat slice of banana bread inside as she said, "to hold you over." Like a metaphor for the hidden wonders of Oakland, Betty's stands unmarked and unlabeled on the corner of Telegraph and 51st. Betty came from Australia to cook at Chez Panisse for three years before opening this small bakery. Her talent shines through in each sandwich and cake. The menu is simple, and there are only a few stools on which to savor a fried chicken sandwich or a slice of her delicious rhubarb pie. Try a scone or brownie for a morning treat or one of Betty's lemon bars that are so rich you should split one with a friend. She and her staff have genuine smiles on their faces and are on a first name basis with many of their customers. The sandwiches aren't served until 11 or 11:30. If there's no sitting room they'll pack up anything picnic style. You can also get a taste at their stalls at Walnut Creek, Danville, and Alameda Farmers Markets.

Tamarindo Antojeria Mexicana

468 8th Street at Washington Street
444.1944
www.tamarindoantojeria.com
Open: Tu-Th 11a-3p, 5-930p; F 11a-3p, 5-10p, Sat 10a-10p,
Sun-M Closed
$$ Ro Fr Vtn

Take a taco, add a dash of class and a smidgeon of modern flair and you get Tamarindo, a year-old Mexican eatery in Old Oakland. A festive tapas menu for lunch transforms into a multi-course dinner listing and starched linens are brought out. Locally raised meats and mostly organic produce brighten the tastes of the already inventive incarnations of Mexican classics. The sopecitos are a trio of masa corn cakes, decked out with a warming chorizo-potato mixture, spicy carnitas and a melt-in-your mouth combination of rajas, fresh corn and cotija cheese. An array of add-ons gives the menu a mix and match feel. I paired a bouquet of grilled peppers with cooling ceviche, and their unparalleled Mexican rice (not dry at all) with crispy tacos de camaron, stuffed with tender rock shrimp. Salsa and soups are very spicy, too spicy even for some who usually take the heat. All's well that ends well, so finish your dining experience with the creamiest flan I've had this side of the border.

The Golden Lotus

1301 Franklin Street at 13th Street
893.0383
Open: M-Sun 11a-9p
$ Vtn Vn

This all-vegetarian restaurant is a true gem. No meat, no poultry, no MSG—all a bargain price! Don't be confused by menu options like beef broccoli or Kung Pao chicken, its all soy or gluten, though your taste buds would have you believe otherwise.

Le Cheval

1007 Clay Street at 9th Street
763.8495
www.lecheval.com
Open: M-Sat 11a-930p, Sun 5-930p
$$ Fam Vtn

Every shade of skin, from every ethnicity can be found chowing down on this authentically delicious Vietnamese cuisine. Great cheap lunch deals, Monday through Saturday, and clay pots for nightly dinner, make Le Cheval's the clear favorite for Vietnamese in Oakland. The salt and pepper prawns and famous carrot chowder are a must. Le Cheval is a staple for an Old Oakland luncheon.

Phnom Penh House

251 8th Street at Harrison Street
893.3825
Open: M-Th 11a-915p, F-Sat 11a-945p
$$ Ro

This is Cambodian food at its best. Phnom Penh is not just another hole-in-the-wall; it's the one that leads to a treasure chest of tasty treats. Cambodia's hot weather and abundant produce influence the cuisine in a refreshing way. The crepe appetizer is filled with sizzling meat and crunchy bean sprouts with a delightful chili sauce. Hot BBQ chicken comes several different ways. Light zesty palates and flavorful vegetarian dishes mix with an assortment of curries, mostly steeped with coconut milk. The salads are a real winner, and cheap too. If you've never had Cambodian, you have to try it, and this is exactly the place to do it.

Genova Delicatessen

5095 Telegraph Avenue at 51st Street
652.7401
Open: M-Sat 8a-7p, Sun 8a-6p
$ S Fr Fam Vtn

Genova's creates personalized sandwiches from an array of snazzy ingredients. Slop a pile of New York style coleslaw on your roast beef, or try one of the varieties of prosciutto. Pick your bread—the ciabatta is my favorite—and your own heap of fillings. Authentic Italian pasta and white beans are also available in their grocery section.

Arizmendi, Lakeshore Avenue

Arizmendi

3265 Lakeshore Avenue at Lake Park Avenue
268.8849
Open: M 7a-3p, Tu-Sat 7a-7p
(Pizza 1130a until closing)
$ Vtn S Fr

Everyday there is a new, exciting pizza and an original loaf of bread. Toppings include everything from yams to shallots to walnuts, and yes, this is real Californian pizza, so don't go expecting deep dish Chicago. A blend of cheese and herbs on crispy thin crust makes each interesting combination worth a try. I've positively fallen for the leek variations, who knew? The breads are as good; bring home the cherry corn scones, or try a *chocolate thing* for a sweet tooth breakfast. Arizmendi also hosts pizza parties for school kids; the twist is the class has to grow its own pizza toppings.

Uncle Willie's Bar-BQ and Fish
614 14ᵗʰ Street at Jefferson Street
465.9200
www.unclewilliesbarbq.com
Open: M-Sat 11a-9p
$ S Fr

Barbequing hat donned, Uncle Willie himself can be found mixing up some of his spicy sauce in the back. His fried chicken wings and pork ribs are the best things on the menu. The greens are soft and not too tangy. What he considers a sandwich is really a huge plate of barbequed meat with some slices of bread on the side. One order is more than enough for two, just watch out for the spicy sauce, it means business.

Los Comales
2105 MacArthur Boulevard at Dimond Avenue
531.3660
Open: M-Sat 10a-9p
$ Fam S

People may think I am overdoing it when I pile my tray with extra salsa cups, but at Los Comales I am welcomed as one of the gang. I can pour their fresh homemade salsas on my gourmet veggie burrito, filled with grilled veggies and guacamole, or a chile relleño burrito. The verde sauce is mild and fruity, the chipotle is toasty and the habanero type is hotter than hot. These salsas make an already stupendous burrito even more so. They even grill jalapenos with those cute crisscross grill marks; take the seeds out to tone the heat down.

World Cup Coffee Tamales
1212 Fruitvale Avenue at International Boulevard
436.7455
Open: M-Sat 7a-6p
$ Fr

Don't be confused by the name, World Cup Coffee makes the best tamales around. The Tamale Queen, as she is lovingly called, grills the chilies and pork and rolls the puffy corn meal mix into their individual sheaths right in the back patio. Every order is steamed fresh. This is an authentic way to try Mexican food, complete with the family feeling of the café.

IB's
1601 San Pablo at 16th Street
839.5018
Open: M-F 10a-4p
$ Fr

Though IB's is of East Coast originthe hoagies and cheese steaks have undergone a California hybridization. My friends and I have had oodles of fun coming up with a name for the hoagie-steak blend they serve. (Among my favorites are hosteak and cheesetoagie). My loyalty to IB's is sealed with the 1.99 bucket of canola-fried French fries, or their cheese curly fries. The prices are right and the food is hot and satisfying, and served with a smile. Happy cooks make good food.

B
499 9th Street at Washington Street
251.8770
www.b-oakland.com
Open: Tu-F 1130a-3p, Tu-Th 530-930p & F-Sat 530-1030p
$$$ Ro PW Vtn

B is a real city place. Every great city has them—that rustic chic-meets-business cool of a restaurant. The salads and sandwiches are a delightful entrée into lunch. Lightly and tastefully dressed, organic or sustainably-grown and well-paired tastes make a very good lunch menu. Some particularly well-designed dishes are the wild boar ragù with truffle oil and pasta, the golden beet salad with goat cheese and fennel, and the boxed chicken sandwich with walnut pesto and green apples. The raspberry lemonade is first class.

Hang Out

All the best chill out spots, from a cozy reading nook to a relaxed microbrew with your buddies

Spud's Pizza, Adeline Street

Sometimes the best way to get a sense of a place is to slow down and stop attempting to see everything and do everything. California is known for its relaxed pace of life, so take the chance to get into it yourself. Read some Gary Schneider poems with a cup of fair-trade cappuccino; put your feet up and play board games. Forget your worries and take a moment to just enjoy the simple things in life.

Spud's Pizza
3290 Adeline Street at Alcatraz Avenue
597.0795
www.spudspizza.net
www.spudstravels.com
Open: M-Th & Sun 7a-9p, F-Sat 7a-10p
$ Fr Vtn Fam WiFi

Spud's provides not only free WiFi, but the computers as well, not to mention the delicious thin-crust pizza. Crispy and covered with whatever toppings your heart desires, Spud's pizzas are one of a kind. Next to the pizza counter is a café with coffee and baked treats to suit your mood. Ask for coupon deals to get an extra discount at the register.

Cato's Ale House
3891 Piedmont Avenue at Montell Street
655.3349
Open: M-F 1130a-10p, Sat-Sun 1130a-11p
$ WiFi Fr

This place exemplifies the laid-back tavern. Free WiFi and live bluegrass accompany the wide assortment of microbrews. There's never any cover charge, and most Wednesday and Sundays bands play everything from Latin to Folk. Tuesdays certain beers are featured, a great time to save a buck and try something new.

Nomad Café
6500 Shattuck Avenue at Alcatraz Avenue
595.5344
www.nomadcafe.net
Open: M-Sat 7a-10p, Sun 8a-10p
$ WiFi S Vtn Vn

Organic fair-trade coffee, free WiFi and a few shelves of interesting books draw a nice crowd of morning caffeine lovers, writers, and neighborhood people. Nomad is a great spot to chill out, put your feet up or sit in the sun at one of their street-side tables.

Fenton's Creamery

4226 Piedmont Avenue at Gleneden Avenue
658.7000
www.fentonscreamery.com
Open: M-Th & Sun 11a-11p, F-Sat 11a-12p
$$ Fam Fr

The legacy of Fenton's has reached its 110th year, and the crowds are still coming. Aside from the classic banana split, there are fanciful sundaes and ice cream flavors that have stayed in the family since the first time Fenton's served ice cream. Rocky Road, Swiss Milk Chocolate and Toasted Almond are originals, and share the menu with seasonal flavors like apple pie and pumpkin, all made in house. After you have your cone in hand, you can take a tour of the creamery process. During dinnertime you may have to wait, Fenton's also served diner mainstays, all prepared without trans-fats.

Parkway Theater

1834 Park Boulevard at E 18th Street
848.1994
www.picturepubpizza.com

Take a break from the multiplex and see a film from the vantage point of a comfy loveseat or sofa. Put your feet up and munch on some tasty popcorn or right-out-of-the-oven pizza. Enjoy a free screening and discussion group with local activist and community organizations at the weekly Sunday Salon. Sip on a pint of beer while you reminisce on old Looney Toons. There are any number of things the regulars love about the Parkway Theater, my personal favorite is Wednesday two-for-one night: two people go to the movies for 5 bucks!

Parkway Theater, Park Boulevard

Prism Café

1918 Park Boulevard at E 19th Street
251-1453
www.prismcafe.com
Open: M-Th 7a-10p, F 7a-Midnight, Sat 8a-Midnight,
Sun 8a-10p

Prism Café is a relaxing place to gather your thoughts or munch on a grilled veggie panini or an organic hummus plate. Comfortable lounge chairs and sofas encircle a small stage where local performers and open mic nights entertain. I like to get a warm mug of organic mocha made with both fair-trade hot chocolate and coffee after a show at the Parkway a few doors down.

Deep Roots Urban Teahouse

1418 34th Avenue at International Boulevard
436.0121
Open: Tu-Sat 11a-7p, Sun 12a-5p

For organic teas, vegan paninis and tasty salads, Deep Roots fits the bill. Try a hot fusion of flavors while you relax in this city oasis. They host a wide variety of music and art events, as well as gatherings of forward-thinking community members. With 40 varieties of tea, a comfy atmosphere, and a strong social ethic, this café really strikes a chord with the positive rejuvenation of Oakland.

Mama Buzz Café

2318 Telegraph Avenue at 23rd Street
465.4073
www.mamabuzzcafe.com
Open: M-Th 7a-9p, F-Sat 7a-10p, Sun 8a-9p

Coffee and art house by day, live performances by night, this fringe-style café hosts the hot and the hip.

L'Amyx Tea Bar

4179 Piedmont Avenue at Linda Avenue
594.8322
www.lamyx.com
Open: M-F 11a-Midnight, Sat-Sun 10a-Midnight
$ S

Work on your latest poem while sipping on a rare tisane and savoring part of the local art scene. L'Amyx has a three-page menu with teas from all the corners of the world. A relaxed atmosphere make it a great place to get creative and get into the community of tea drinkers.

Casual Night Out

Dining and delighting in a relaxed atmosphere

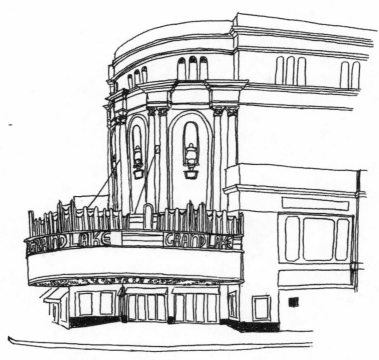

Grand Lake Theater, Grand Avenue

There is always a time when you just want to kick back, and have a relaxed evening out. In fact, Californians are known the world over for their propensity towards all things casual. Go out, but go in comfort, with the divine purpose of repose. Good eats, good laughs and films galore lie ahead.

Grand Lake Theater

3200 Grand Avenue at Lake Park Avenue
452.3556
www.renaissancerialto.com/current/grandlake.htm

Owner and operator Allen Michaan has gone well beyond a basic refurbishment at this historical venue; it has become his hobby. He displays his collection of classic film projectors in a corridor of this 1926 theater, which originally played silent movies and vaudeville shows. Extraordinary examples of Tiffany glass adorn the walls. Michaan's forward political views are posted next to movie titles on the highly visible marquee. He has hung genuine Persian carpets from the walls of the Persian theater, and hired an archeologist to paint the Hieroglyphs on the walls and ceiling of the Egyptian one. He has poured all his passions into this theater, and you can feel it when you visit. The employees are knowledgeable about the films, and are often ready to strike up a conversation. Saturday nights, before each show there are live Wurlitzer organ concerts, which really take you back in time. Going to the movies should be an event, not a funneling from one line to another. It is a vital part of American culture, and Grand Lake Theater is one of the last places to get that full experience, while seeing the latest films. (For more Tiffany glass, follow Lakeshore Avenue around Lake Merritt to First United Methodist Church, where a number of outstanding Tiffany murals cover the walls.)

Dona Tomas

5004 Telegraph Avenue at 51ˢᵗ Street
New location coming to downtown Oakland soon...
450.0522
Open: Tu-Th 530-930p, F-Sat 530-10p
$$ Fr R Vtn

Dona Tomas allows the true beauty of classic Mexican dishes to resonate; bright colors and distinct flavors abound. Don't miss the appetizers melt-in-your-mouth ceviche and quesadillas made with goat cheese and morels. The meats are well stewed; especially good are the carnitas and mole-drenched chicken. There's also an entire menu dedicated to tequila. Margaritas are as stiff, no substituting agave wine for tequila here. Take the opportunity to elevate your experience of Mexican food by getting a picturesque patio seat at Dona Tomas. The meat and veggies are all organic or sustainably farmed so tasty freshness is undeniable. If you still have any stomach space and are feeling a little adventurous, cap off the evening with one of their interesting desserts. Go out on a limb with the avocado ice cream, or finish your meal with a sensuous bowl of Mexican hot chocolate.

On Screen In Oakland

Screenings and film festivals
Paramount Theatre
2025 Broadway at 20ᵗʰ Street
238.4734
www.filmoakland.com

Each week the fabulous Paramount Theatre plays a different film from Hollywood's Golden Era. Don't miss seeing *Gone with the Wind* on the big screen, and nothing beats the ambiance of this classic theater, restored to its full glory. Film Oakland's website also lists all East Bay film festivals, which seem to be nearly continuous. One week it's the Asian International Film Fest, then the Gay and Lesbian, then the Buddhist, then the African American Directors Fest, the list goes on. Check out what will be on screen while you're in town. Outdoor Cinema series is at 9th and Washington during the summer months, and into September.

Flints Bar-B-Q

6609 Shattuck Avenue at 66th Street
595.5323
Open: M-Th 11a-9p, F-Sat 11a-10p, Sun 2-9p
$ Fam

Flint's is the best barbeque in the East Bay, hands down. Served from a tiny hole-in-the-wall on Shattuck, the smokehouse sauce oozes through each juicy morsel. There are four items on the menu: beef links, pork ribs, beef ribs and chicken. They are all good-and come with beans and potato salad. Two orders, about seven bucks a pop, are enough for four average appetites.

Mimosa Café

462 Santa Clara Avenue at Grand Avenue
465.2948
Tu-F 11a-9p Sat 9a-9p, Sun 9a-2p
$$ S Fr Vn Vtn

"Supernatural" by the fading sign outside, Mimosa is a true gem among Oakland restaurants. They have a huge menu satisfying many tastes, like gooey zucchini grilled cheese (stuffed with garlic, sautéed shredded zucchini and a blend of cheeses) and poached fish over brown rice. The dishes are simple yet well done, utilizing French cooking methods. You can have a healthy meal out and enjoy it too. Don't pass up their outstanding Sunday brunch.

Oliveto, College Avenue

Oliveto Downstairs & Cafe

5655 College Avenue at Shafter Avenue
547.5356
www.oliveto.com
Open: M 7a-9p, Tu-F 7a-10p, Sat 8a-10p, Sun 8a-9p
$$$ Ro R Vtn

Just on a whim you can muster up a mighty meal at Oliveto Downstairs, the more casual sister of Oliveto Restaurant (see **Dress Up** chapter). Grab a swanky version of the classic hamburger with a sudsy pint. Or try one of the premier wood oven specialties like Cornish hen or pigeon. Wear jeans while you pick at the finest antipasto served in Oakland. No reservations needed. All the pastas are handmade that evening, but the wood oven spit yields the best dishes in the house.

Jesso's

901 Washington Street at 9th Street
451.1561
www.jessos.com
Open: M-Th Noon-1230a, F-Sat Noon-1a, Sun 3-1130p
$$ Fam

Jesso's menu is full of choices. The grilled option for fish dishes brings out the plump loveliness of catfish, rarely paralleled. The hushpuppies are irresistible and the collards (they cook them with catfish broth) and candied yams are quite good. Spicy Cajun fries are excellent dipped in house-made coleslaw. Jesso's is a successful example of a family owned restaurant. It is hard to find a table on the weekend for the live blues and R&B they host. On a summer evening make sure to get a sidewalk table.

Pizzaiolo

5008 Telegraph Avenue at 51st Street
652.4888
www.pizzaiolo.us
Open: Tu-Sat 530-10p
$$ Fr PW Vtn

I believe the saying goes something like, 'go to California, but leave before it makes you too soft, go to New York, but leave before it makes you too hard.' I don't know where you are supposed to go after that. Pizzaiolo strives to bring that be-there-or-be-square toughness of New York into their Telegraph Avenue restaurant. The perpetual lines of people hovering outside look as though they are secretly hoping to get their snap shot in the seen-around-town section of some glossy Long Island magazine. It takes me back. But out of this hybrid sort of coolness comes an elegant whisper of a pizza. Delicate flavors dance on a crispy thin crust. The finest olives and anchovies or wild rocket and house-made sausage make robust pairings on smooth goat's milk ricotta, baked in the fiery brick oven. An assortment of other toppings can be sampled on their ever-changing menu. Fresh made pasta and a few meat or fish selections make a more substantial meal. Pizzaiolo is really all about the pizza, and I would recommend sticking with it. A clear exception to this rule however, are the soups, sheer and unwavering bliss. All ingredients are locally and sustainably farmed. Wear jeans and shiny shoes and get there before 5:30 to wait on one of the sidewalk benches—they take no reservations.

Mijori
3260 Grand Avenue at Lake Park Avenue
510.465.8854
Open: M-Sat 1130a-230p, 5-930p
$ Fr

Cheap, fresh sushi, served in imaginative ways–that is the bottom line at Mijori's. Believe it, even at reasonable prices, this place has a very high standard of freshness. Go ahead, dive into the raw! The marinated shitake rolls are tops, and they are only a couple bucks. Mijori's serves the best lion roll around (California roll topped with salmon sashimi and sauce then baked). The house-made vegetable gyoza are unbelievable, and are a great prelude to one of their creative rolls, like the Y2K or the caterpillar. This business has stayed in the family since its opening some 20 years ago, you can even meet the owner in person on his day off. Join in by sampling one of their many quality sakes, and if you need to chill out afterward, head a block down the street to the Grand Lake Theater.

Koryo Wooden Charcoal B.B.Q.
4390 Telegraph Avenue at 44th Street
6526007
Open: Everyday 11a-2a
$$ Fr Fam

Although Oakland's weather is usually welcoming and warm, there are those chilly nights where the breeze goes up your spine and gives you a shiver. That is when I head to Koryo, where two orders of their marinated beef will get me a grill-side seat and the tastiest way to warm up. Number 31 or 32 on the menu are the short cut to grilling your own meal. Hot embers enclosed in a mesh grill arrive at the table and warm you while you cook. When the thinly sliced meat grills through, you can eat it with any number of vegetables and sauces, including four types of kimchee. The pancake appetizer goes perfectly in this mix of spicy, salty and sweet. No other Korean barbeque in the Bay Area comes close.

Café Van Kleef

1621 Telegraph Avenue at 16th Street
763.7711
www.cafevankleef.com
Open: M-F 4p-2a, Sat 6p-2a, Sun 8p-2a

Much all of Oakland agrees: Van Kleefs' is the best bar around. The visionary artist owner has dreamt up a dazzling space that is anything but boring. The Greyhounds are known across the Bay, made from Grey Goose and fresh squeezed grapefruit juice. If that isn't your bag, any of the citrus-based cocktails are just as fresh, and mix well with a cool crowd and the lull of Edith Piaf or the twang of Elvis that plays when there isn't a live band. Funky local art completes the scene, where Jerry Brown and his cohorts are known to frequent. Free parking is around the corner at 17th and Broadway, convenient when you forget when street cleaning commences. 19th Street BART stop is right there too.

Everett and Jones BBQ

126 Broadway at Embarcadero West, 2676 Fruitvale Avenue at East 27th Street and 1955 San Pablo Avenue at University Avenue
663.2350
www.eandjbbq.com
Open: M-Th 11a-10p, F 11a-Midnight, Sat-Sun 12p-Midnight
$$ Fam

A true meat lover's paradise, these are some dynamite ribs. The spicy barbeque sauce is a family recipe generations-old, that drips into every slow-cooked morsel of meat. Be prepared for an après-dining bath! The sides are good too, as is the Saucey Sistah Ale. But nothing is prepared without meat, or meat juices, so don't try to bring your vegetarian friends along, unless they don't mind just coming for the cornbread, ice tea and nightly live blues.

A single mother of nine, who thought her tasty barbeque secrets could support her growing children, opened this place. And boy was she right. The Everett and Jones dynasty began, and has been known for the best brisket ever since. The fearlessness she demonstrated by opening her own business, in the face of all obstacles has brought genuine heart into this city, a real blessing.

New World Vegetarian

464 8th Street at Broadway
444.2891
www.themenupage.com/newworldvegetarian.html
Open: Sun-Thurs 11a-9p, Fri-Sat 11a-930p
$ Vn

Vegan food is usually a hard sell for carnivores, but New World is a hit with all sorts of eaters. Their dishes represent an array of international cuisines. Wet burritos stuffed with fresh grilled veggies are served on the same table as a platter of rice paper wraps doused with a divine peanut sauce. Scrumptious vegan chicken nuggets, sesame glazed tofu and stir-fried (vegan) beef provide enough protein for any red-blooded man. The high point of the menu was the surprisingly flavorful Thai fish patties, served with pungent sauce and crispy veggies. Sour cream cake with coconut and vegan cream cheese icing rivals its dairy competitors. The servers are observant and quiet, helping to complete a peaceful mealtime atmosphere.

Listen

Any auditory experience you can imagine, from festivals, comedy clubs, open mics to headlining shows– it's all here

Oakland Metro, Broadway

Well-strung notes can carry every shade of human emotion. I like to close my eyes and let my other senses go when I catch wind of some magical melodies. My mother used to say you can't listen with your mouth open. But some of these places promote listening while you eat scrumptious tapas or sashimi. Whatever your ears perk up to, it is essential to enjoy sounds and indulge in it as often as possible.

Tourettes Without Regrets

The Oakland Metro
201 Broadway at 2nd Street
Info: tongueartillery@yahoo.com
First Thursday of every month, 830p
Sign up to perform at 8p
$7 at the door

Okay, it has a funny name, but this is one of the premier poetry slams and emcee battles in the state. The mission is to bring together fearless poets and rhymers, and give a voice to the people. Slam poetry is a powerful way to communicate deep sorrows, great joys, perseverance and peace. The hip-hop movement actually has little to do with the gangs in the news, and more to do with turning something bad into something good. (Lets think back to slavery and the blues for a moment...) Many nationally-known freestlyers and poets got their start here, and are now touring or are on stage at the HBO Def Jam poetry slam. I've even gotten on stage, and had a chance to perform. Just be aware that this event is loud, and clearly identifies the generation gap.

Eli's Mile High Club

3629 Martin Luther King Jr. Way at 36th Street
654.4549
www.oaklandmilehigh.com
Open: 6p-Midnight

Home to the best blues in the East Bay, this small and funky venue looks like a southern roadhouse, with the goods inside. Don't go for a chic night out, go for the music. Soulful blues are on the bill every night it's open, weekends and some Thursdays. Check the website for up-to-date schedules.

Club Anton

428 3rd Street at Broadway
463.0165
www.clubanton.com
Open: Th-Sun 7p-2a (21 and over)

This is a snazzy club where it is easy to get caught up in deep hip-hop rhythms or Latin beats. The crowd is fun loving and serious about the music, more so than at other bars in the area.

The Ruby Room

132 14th Street at Madison Street
444.7224
Open: M-Sun 5p-2a

Step back in time into the 50's at this rosy lounge, teeming with cheap drinks. On Monday nights at midnight Old Crow shots are only 1 dollar. Honky tonk tunes, punk, and an eclectic assemblage of beats spin between the pleather seating and an exposed rock wall. Wednesday night British invasion strikes with a vengeance.

Woodminster Summer Musicals

3300 Joaquin Miller Road at Crane Way
531.9597, 531.0671
www.woodminster.com

Grab the family and your comfy clothes for an outdoor treat. A full season of different musicals shows in this park amphitheater throughout the summer months. Groups get half price tickets and kids are always free. These dramatic concerts are a favorite with locals, and are great fun for families who want to relax and enjoy a genuine summer outing in the Oakland hills.

Four Seasons Concerts

601.7919
Several locations

Featuring unique performers, both young and old, and from all different backgrounds, the Four Seasons Concert series brings quality classical music to the community. If you drive a senior citizen who is a season ticket holder to the show you get free tickets to see the concert, a great incentive and also a wonderful way to meet fellow appreciators of fine music. Concerts are held at different theaters throughout the concert season, which ranges from early Fall through the Spring. Among the venues are Herbst Theater (in San Francisco), Regents Theater at Holy Names University, Roda Theater at the Berkeley Repertory Theater, and Calvin Simmons Theater near Lake Merrit.

Temescal Café Wednesday Comedy Night
Temescal Café, Telegraph Avenue at 49th Street
Starts at 8p

Temescal Café hosts an uproarious Comedy Night every Wednesday that has garnered several prizes as best local comedy night around. Check out all kinds of acts, from amateur (Ben Franklin pointed out this word actually refers to a person who truly loves what he or she does...) to professional. Other nights there is a mix of music; some good some bad, but there is never any cover charge. (See **Up Early** chapter.)

La Taza de Café
3909 Grand Avenue at Sunny Slope Avenue
658.2373
Open: Tu-Th & Sun 5-1030p, F-Sat 5p-Midnight,
Sat-Sun 10a-2p
$$ Ro

This new tapas place is a great way to enjoy chic gourmet foods for less moolah. Most of the dishes are under 12 dollars. Another plus is La Taza hosts hard-to-find Cuban salsa every Thursday night, and belly dancing on Fridays. Weekends include a host of authentic Latin performers in the upstairs section. While you listen, try the pincho beef or the chicken skewers, both served on arepas (traditional corn cakes). This place is sure to lift your spirits-just make sure you have enough energy to last the night!

Paramount Theatre, Broadway

Paramount Theatre

2025 Broadway at 20th Street
465.6400
www.paramounttheatre.com

This National Historic Landmark is one of the finest examples of Art Deco architecture, designed by Timothy L. Pflueger. After an authentic and extensive restoration in the early 1970's, the theater is now host to the Oakland Ballet, The Oakland East Bay Symphony, the Oakland Interfaith Gospel Choir as well as other performers and films.

Yoshi's

510 Embarcadero West at Washington Street
238.9200
www.yoshis.com
Open: M-F 1130a-2p, Sun Noon-2p, M-Th & Sun 530-10p,
F-Sat 530-11p
$$ Ro S Vtn

Yoshi's is the Blue Note of the West Coast. Called "a sanctuary of jazz" by drumming great Billy Higgins, top names as well as local talents are featured 363 days of the year. The Bay Area fosters some of the most forward jazz programs for youth in the country, thus high school bands and locals that get to start out at Yoshi's often end up touring the world. It is one thing to be the top place in the Bay Area to hear jazz, it is entirely another to be creating a culture of jazz by supporting the up and coming musicians. The preservation of this wildly freeing form of music is paramount, so I join Yoshi's in celebrating it as much as possible. Shows are usually 8pm and 10pm. I strongly recommend dropping in at 6pm for the early show to reserve your seats. Then you can go out for dinner and not have to worry about being stuck in the back corner when it's time for the music. The nosh is great, small sushi and Asian-inspired tapas accompany the music. I love the gyoza chips. For bigger names reserve tickets in advance, but many weekday shows can be an impromptu rendezvous with live jazz at an affordable price.

Dress Up

Don your shiny shoes and head out to one of these fancy places, not all come with a huge price tag

Air, 9th Street

There are those occasions where you just have to dress up—something inside you wants to put your good foot forward and go all out. These spots are as fancy as Oakland gets, and that isn't that fancy. The laid-back dress code has spread all over the state of California, and has been especially relaxed in the north. But if you are looking for an opportunity to take your new dress shoes out on the town, these places are your best bet. Not everywhere requires big bucks, though some are pricier. Remember drinks are usually the culprit for amping up your dining bill, so if you are careful in that department you can make even the more expensive places affordable.

Air Lounge

492 9th Street at Clay Street
385.7568
www.airoakland.com
Open: Th-Sat 5p-2a
$$ Fr S

Air isn't the kind of place you'd expect to find in Oakland, but then again, I always expect the unexpected in this city. With designer lighting and a phenomenally New York feel, and New York prices, Air is the best bar for schmoozing in your coolest duds.

Luka's Tap Room and Bar

2221 Broadway at Grand Avenue
451.4677
Open: M-F 1130a-230p, Everyday 530p-1030p, Sun 11a-3p
(Bar menu after lunch and after dinner until midnight)
$$ Fr

Luka's is one of the many signs of rejuvenation in downtown Oakland. Serving lunch and dinner. It is home to 16 beers and a snazzy dance floor, this place offers a complete night out. You might even catch a glimpse of one of Oakland's professional athletes.

Oliveto, College Avenue

Oliveto Restaurant

5655 College Avenue at Shafter Avenue
547.5356
www.oliveto.com
Open: M-F 1130a-2p, M 530-9p, Tu-W 530-930p,
Th-Sat 530-10p, Sun 5-9p
$$$ Ro PW Vtn

What's the greatest thing about Oliveto? It may sound surprising—but I'd say the value. For the same price as one of the many sub-par Italian restaurants in the Bay Area, you can have the finest braised rabbit or handmade gnocchi that melts in your mouth. Try the astonishingly smooth and rich tasting pâté plate.

On weekday nights it isn't so overcrowded that you need a reservation. None of the snobbery that exists at other genuine fine dining places manifests itself here—and yet the food definitely reaches the highest standards. The entrees at the more fancy upstairs range from 16-30 dollars. Don't assume you can't afford to have the finest food. Yes, it is one of the best restaurants in the Bay Area, but no, it doesn't have a months-long waiting list, red tape or a retentive dress code. Eat at home for a week or two to save up, then come here and manifest your incarnation as royalty. One of the owners did her doctorate on olives. You can be sure every detail has been selectively chosen, including the table olives.

TJ's Gingerbread House

741 5th Street at Brush Street
444.7373
www.tjsgingerbread.com/
Open: Tu-Sat 11a-730p or later
$$ Fam

TJ's is a grand restaurant, like none other. Crouched beneath the BART tracks and the 880 Highway, the restaurant has remained in the same location through Oakland's many incarnations. Decorated like a living ginger bread house, both inside and out, TJ herself has created a dream-like paradise, and a menu to set it apart. Reservations are necessary for several of the dishes, like the Louisiana Fancy Fine Jumbo and the Catfish Étouffée. Each meal comes with several courses. The best thing on the menu is the sassy cornbread, possibly the best in the world, which comes with any order. Gingerbread houses are made during the holidays, but you can get the cookies, even chocolate chip ginger cookies, all year long.

À Côté

5478 College Avenue at Taft Avenue
655.6469
Open: Sun-Tu 530-10p, W-Th 530-11p, F-Sat 530p-Midnight,
Sun 10a-2p
$$ Fr Vtn

Dubbed the best place for cocktails in the East Bay, À Côté serves fanciful drinks made with fine spirits and fresh juices. Their notable French tapas, and extraordinary pommes frites are practically addictive. This is chi chi gourmet for the next generation, well the ones with good jobs that is.

Montclair Bistro

6118 Medau Place at Moraga Avenue
482.8282
www.montclairbistro.com
Open: Tu-Th & Sun 6-9p, F-Sat 6-930p, Tu-F & Sun 1130a-2p
$$ Fam Vtn

For more conservative taste buds, Montclair Bistro serves traditional steaks and smart fish dishes. This is simple and classic fare done in a way that can accommodate even the pickiest of eaters.

Bay Wolf

3853 Piedmont Avenue at Rio Vista Avenue
655.6004
www.baywolf.com
Open: M-F 1130a-145p, F-Sat 530-10p Sun-Th 530-930p (closing times may vary)
$$$ Fr Ro Vtn Vn

Ranked 4th in the prestigious *SF Guardian*'s annual "Top 100 Restaurants of the Bay", Bay Wolf has been quietly creating culinary magic for almost 30 years. A seamless blend of Mediterranean and Californian cuisine, the highlight is certainly the tender rack of lamb and the unimaginably delicious deserts. The beef pot roast rises above the competition. Any guy who takes his gal here is a keeper.

Citron

5484 College Avenue at Taft Avenue
653-5484
Open: Tu-F 1130a-430p, M-Tu 530-9p, W-Th 530-930p,
Fr 530-10p, Sat 5-10p, Sun 5-9p
$$$ Ro Fr Vtn

Attention to detail is the name of the game here at Citron. A crew of servers wait on your every need, they even hold the door open for you at the restroom. After a few minutes at the table you are gifted with a complimentary bouchée (a pre-appetizer) to whet your appetite. Simple and elegant meat and fish dishes are coupled with sublime vegetables roasted and pureed. You can opt for their 3-5 course tasting menus, though the portions are a tad smaller than a la carte. It is one of the few places in Oakland where almost everyone is wearing a proper jacket, but the place is kept so warm, I don't know how the guys can manage it comfortably.

Di Bartolo Restaurant

3310 Grand Avenue at Mandana Boulevard
832.9005
Open: Tu-Sun 530-1030p, bar stays open until midnight
$$$ Fr Vtn

The brand new restaurant, opened by the same owner as the coffee shop next door, is simply blissful. Imaginative mixed drinks are served strong. Fish is cooked perfectly. Fusion cuisine is minimized with a menu focused on northern Spanish and Italian dishes. Plates are distinctive, layered with complementary flavors. Come for tapas and drinks, pizza and hard-to-find Belgian beers, or an out and out feast. The desserts cannot be skipped. Chocolate is elevated to manna; pana cotta dazzled with strawberry juice is mind-altering. This restaurant hits all the marks.

Pearl Oyster Bar

5634 College Avenue at Shafter Avenue
654.5426
www.pearloncollege.com
Open: Sun-Th 530-10p, F-Sat 530p-Midnight
(Bar menu F-Sat after 10p)
$$ Fr Vtn

Let me tell you about the sturgeon I ordered at Pearl: crusted in a ground cacao, coffee and cardamom bouquet, poached delicately and perched atop a magnificent cauliflower puree and red wine emulsion—I was dumbfounded. Sophisticated, yes, but this dish was pure genius. Pearl has that certain *je ne sais quoi* some other seafood restaurants can only hope for.

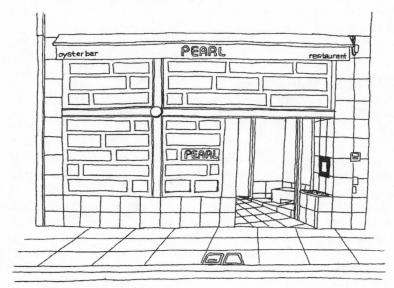

Pearl, College Avenue

Get Inspired

Museums, installations, awe-inspiring exhibits and anything that aims to enthuse

Oakland Museum of California, Oak Street

Oakland has been a haven for the arts for over 100 years. Dance, blues, sculpture, literature, painting, architecture, hip-hop and film— Oakland's art scene has been intertwined with a full spectrum of mediums throughout various movements. Connecting with the deep undercurrents of social justice, eloquent beauty and passionate reformation completes the picture of Oakland as a city, both past and present. Here is a listing of galleries and museums that bring to surface the artistic integrity of this part of the world.

Oakland Museum of California

1000 Oak Street at 10th Street
238.2200
www.museumca.org
Open: W-Sat 10a-5p, Sun Noon-5p
(1st Friday of the month, until 9p)

The Oakland Museum of California is the kind of museum children grow up in. The permanent exhibits on natural habitats and geography become familiar pleasures; the shifting ones bring new excitement. Take part in one of the many annual festivals that the museum hosts throughout the year. (See the **Calendar** in the **Introduction** for more information). Street parking can sometimes be difficult and the museum's garage is expensive. The Lake Merritt BART station is directly across from the museum, so it is the most convenient way to get there.

African American Museum and Library at Oakland

659 14th Street at Martin Luther King Jr. Way
637.0200
www.oaklandlibrary.org/AAMLO
Open: Tu-Sat Noon-530p

This unique branch of the large Oakland library system houses an extensive collection of historic papers, books and documents about African American people and their profound achievements. On the second floor is a real gem of a museum where there is always some interesting historical display or art exhibit. Community art projects and exposés on important leaders and pioneers make this an important place to visit in Oakland. The library itself is beautiful, one of the Carnegie famous projects.

Oakland ART Gallery

199 Kahn's Alley, Frank H. Ogawa Plaza at Broadway
637.0395
www.oaklandartgallery.org
Open: W-Th 11a-6p, F 11a-5p, Sat Noon-5p

This is a non-profit gallery that has wonderful shows of both emerging and established artists. Some pieces I have seen here tended toward the wacky end of the spectrum, but I have been pleasantly surprised. It is a fun place to pop your head in when you are in Frank H. Ogawa Plaza.

Association of Clay and Glass Artists of California

General Info: (925) 254.8457
www.acga.net

ACGA offers classes, shows, publications, and a library of resources. Rotating shows circulate throughout the Bay Area; many find a home in Oakland's galleries. Check the website for up-to-date information.

State of California Craft and Cultural Arts Gallery

1515 Clay Street Atrium at 15th Street
622.8190
CCAGallery@mail2Art.com
www.oaklandculturalarts.org
Open: M-F 10a-5p

Located in the airy atrium of Oakland's government complex, the Craft and Cultural Art Gallery brings to life the different movements in music, painting and culture that has taken place in Oakland. It is the best place to delve into local history through art. Afterwards go for a snack at the café upstairs and you might be able to strike up a conversation with the local politicians.

Thelma Harris Galleries

5940 College Avenue at Chabot Road
654-0443
Open: Tu-F 11a-6p, Sat Noon-5p

I highly recommend this straight ahead gallery, where I have seen some of the best painting shows in the Bay Area.

Mills College Art Museum

Aron Art Center
5000 MacArthur Boulevard at Richards Road
430.2164
www.mills.edu/campus_life/art_museum/
Open: Tu 11a-4p, Wed 11a-730p, Th-Sat 11a-4p,
Sun Noon-4p

This gallery and museum features the works of students, and resident artists as well as nationally known collections.

Museum of Children's Art (MOCHA)

538 9th Street at Clay Street
465.8770
www.mocha.org
Open: Tu-F 10a-5p, Sat-Sun 12a-5p

With a mission to bring art in to children's lives, MOCHA has hands-on exhibits that excite the artistic side of young people's minds. The art is largely interactive, and kid-friendly. You can touch the art, instead of being separated from it by glass and fancy alarm systems. MOCHA's Little Studio (see the **Learn** chapter) gives kids an opportunity to make their own creations after touring through the galleries.

Joyce Gordon Gallery

406 14th Street at Franklin Street
465.8928
www.joycegordongallery.com
Open: W-F 11a-7p, Sat 11a-6p

Newly remodeled, this gallery always has new and thought-provoking displays of paintings and sculptures. The pieces often come with a deeper aim to inspire movement toward a more conscious society. Every fourth Friday, from 7pm, the gallery hosts the "Oakland is a Holy City" poetry and open mic night.

Ebony Art Museum

1034 14th Street at Linden Street
763.0745
Open: Tu-Sat 11a-6p

Explore the rich artistic movements of Africa and its passage and cultural life in America and California. Located across from Lowell Park, the museum is housed in a gated Victorian house, chock full of both pre-colonial African artifacts and modern collections. A recent exhibit entitled Vernita's Soul Food featured collages of dried vegetables and bones, set behind a smattering of black cloth dolls.

Pro Arts

550 2nd Street at Clay Street
763.4361
www.proarts.org
Open: Tu-Sat Noon-6p, Sun Noon-5p

Pro Arts Gallery joins together the area's visual and performing arts venues to offer a unique conversation between ideas and expression. Exhibits at the gallery will be woven into shows at the nearby Metro or Yoshi's. Pro Arts is also the mastermind behind the annual East Bay Open Studios, a two-weekend event that showcases the works of artists around the city. (see **Calendar** for more information.)

Oakland Art Murmur

Between San Pablo Avenue and Telegraph Avenue, 23rd through 33rd Streets
www.oaklandartmurmur.com

The first Friday of every month this eclectic, although somewhat controversial night out is hosted by a group of art galleries in West Oakland, in what is known as the Lower Bottoms district. These new galleries have inspired a monthly art movement, which has turned heads, but may mark the future gentrification of this historic area. Join in, and check it out as one of the venues for Oakland art.

Create

From beads to seeds, fabric to photos, these spots will enable your creative side for sure

I dropped out of college my sophomore year to go to art school. I wanted to draw and paint and take photos all day instead of calculating chemical equations and studying political systems.

Later I changed my mind and went back for international studies and English, but what I learned from the experience was something that hadn't crossed my mind before: everyone can create beauty; everyone really is an artist. I saw people who had never taken their pencil out of the lines on a steno pad draw impeccable contour figures by the end of only one semester. Their eyes and their hands had become one unit. With a little drive anyone can contribute to the beauty in the world. I also feel that it is important to maintain a connection with handwork. If you haven't ever tried something like this yourself, the satisfaction of eating something you have grown or cooked, wearing a dress you made or a scarf you knit is astonishing. Your hands are the greatest machines.

The Knitting Basket

2054 Mountain Boulevard at Antioch Street
www.theknittingbasket.com
339.6295
Open: M-Sat 10a-6p

A full spectrum of colors and textures adorns the shelves of the Knitting Basket. The yarns here are of superior quality. They sell sweaters made by the employees, and offer a range of classes.

Black Dot Arts Collective and Café

1431 23rd Avenue at International Boulevard
532.8559

Local artist and community organizer Marcel Diallo has made it his mission to connect budding artists from the neighborhood with world-renown poets, musicians, thinkers, and creators. His café and collective hosts a variety of events, as well as gallery exhibitions in every medium. 'BeatsFlowsVideos' is an educational program for young emcees to hone their talent after school. Thursday nights at 7pm, they host an open mic at the café. Black Dot has been a guiding light in Oakland's positive growth.

Flowers by Myrna

6200 Antioch Street at Mountain Boulevard
339.0425
Open: M-Sat 830a-630p, Sun 10a-5p

Myrna, another successful female entrepreneur, stocks very high quality flowers, and many unique branches and leaves. It is hard to make a bad arrangement from her selection.

Silkroad Fabric

272 14th Street at Harrison Street
763.1688
www.silkroadfabric.com
Open: M-Sat 10a-7p, Sun 11a-530p

Choose from beautiful silks and bridal fabrics (their specialty), as well as drapery and upholstery textiles at discount prices. They offer the largest variety of rich colors and materials I have seen around the Bay Area.

Discount Fabrics

3006 San Pablo Avenue at Ashby Avenue
548.2981
Open: M-Sat 10a- 6p

Discount Fabrics isn't called that for nothing. Check out the bins towards the front of the store for a slew of great bargains, taffeta for 2 bucks a yard, cheap muslin, funky knits. What the fashion industry refers to as a jobber is often out of reach to the public. Jobbers buy up the leftovers from large manufacturing projects, and sell them at huge reductions. They have a huge section of the store dedicated to upholstery fabrics.

Article Pract

5010 Telegraph Avenue at 50th Street
652.7435
www.articlepract.com
Open: Tu-Th 11a-7p, F-Sun 11a-6p

Yarn made from steel and bamboo? Japanese thread woven from recycled corn silk? No, these are not figments of my imagination; they are actual yarns I have found on the shelves and in the cubbyholes at Article Pract. The rarest and high quality threads aren't always the cheapest, but the final product is much nicer, and longer lasting. Classes in everything from beginning knitting to embossed stitching are continually offered, and when you take a class you get a hefty discount on the yarn.

Rock Paper Scissors

2278 Telegraph Avenue at 23rd Street
238.9171
www.rpscollective.com
Open: Everyday except Tuesday 11a-7p

This local artists' collective believes in sharing skills, resources and time, and has built a creative community stronghold at their Telegraph location. There is studio space where you can give and take classes based on your interests. The place is chock-full of supplies, and when you finish your projects you can sell them on consignment at the front store.

Lacis

2982 Adeline Street at Ashby Avenue
843.7290
Info: rebecca@lacis.com
Open: M-F 1-530p, Sat 11a-530p

An incredible inventory of lace making tools and textile related books can be found at the aptly named Lacis. Antique findings and unique ribbons, and of course a huge collection of lace make this a national resource for all things frilly.

Snapshot Mosaics

6206 La Salle Avenue at Mountain Boulevard
339.3053
Open: M-Sat 10a-6p, Sun 10a-3p

All the ingredients to start a mosaic project are here at Snapshot. I hadn't realized how much more there was to mosaics than floors and walls. You can make exquisite earrings or a sturdy tabletop from these small pieces of art glass. There is gallery space, ready-made pieces; as well as all the necessary supplies at this locally owned small business.

Piedmont Stationers

4171 Piedmont Avenue at Linda Avenue
655.2375
Open: M-F 930a-6p, Sat 10a-6p, Sun Noon-5p

This is a nice neighborhood stationer, where you can find cool pens and papers, art supplies, and filing supplies for any number of creative endeavors. The prices aren't as steep as other small stationers, and you can give yourself a pat on the back for supporting a local business instead of one of the huge office supply conglomerates.

MOCHA Little Studio

538 9th Street at Clay Street
465.8770
hello@mocha.org
www.mocha.org
Open: Tu-Fri 10a-5p, Sat-Sun Noon-5p

This kid's studio features weekly themed projects and all the supplies needed for creativity to flow. For five dollars you can let your child's imagination soar.

Rockridge Library Branch

5366 College Avenue at Manila Avenue
597.5017
Open: M-Tu 1230-8p, W-Th 10a-530p, F Noon-530p,
Sat 10a-530p

The entry way of this particular branch is stacked with generally large piles of free magazines and books that I have turned into some of my best collages. Give it a shot yourself; collage is such a freeing art form.

Poppy Fabrics

5151 Broadway at 51st Street
655.5151
Open: M-F 930a-8p, Sat 930a-530p, Sun 11a-530p

You can imagine dresses and all manner of textile creations from the wide selection of decorator fabrics, fine silks, brocades, and ribbons at Poppy. A highly knowledgeable staff can lead you to the holy grail of the cloth world, whatever that might be for you and your current project. For specific, high quality items, Poppy is the place to go.

Walter Bennett Cameras

3268 Lakeshore Avenue at Lake Park Avenue
893.6960
Open: M-Sat 9a-6p

This local small business carries both digital and film cameras and equipment and is known for professional service and supplies. The beginner and professional are sure to meet at Walter Bennett.

Explore

Places where science is explained, nature abounds or adventure is to be had

Children's Fairyland, Bellevue Avenue

Curiosity can lead down many a path; we've all seen our friend Curious George getting in over his head. But fostering a healthy curiosity about the world is as important as taking our very first steps. If we fill our imagination with programmed images and digital friends, games and life, we miss out on all there is to explore for ourselves. History and science, nature and adventure are waiting around the bend to expand your knowledge of the world around you. Seek out the big questions, ask your own, and most of all enjoy the ride!

Children's Fairyland

699 Bellevue Avenue at Grand Avenue
452.2259
Open: Summer M-F 10a-4p, Sat-Sun 10a-5p (shortened hours in other seasons, open year-round)
Admission: $6, includes unlimited rides, an addition $2 for 'magic keys'

Explore the fairy tales of childhood through rides, interactive displays and live story-telling at the oldest amusement park in the US. Fairyland is home to the longest running puppet theater in America.

Pardee Home

672 11th Street Castro Street
444.2187
info@pardeehome.org
Open: W-F & Sat; tours at Noon, 1, 2 and 3p

On the National Registry of Historic places since the 1970's, this architectural wonder has been restored to its original 1860's glory when a gold miner-turned-eye doctor first built it. His son became the "earthquake governor", who offered safety and shelter to the scores of displaced people in the wake of the 1906 San Francisco earthquake. His wife collected antiques and cultural objects, most of which are still on display in the Pardee home, now an intimate sort of historical museum.

Chabot Space and Science Center

10000 Skyline Boulevard in Redwood Park
336.7300
www.chabotspace.org
Open: Tu-Th 10a-5p, F-Sat 10a-10p, Sun 11a-5p
Admission: $13 adults, $9 kids, $10 students and seniors, additional fees for
special shows

Exhibitions on planetary movement, stars, the universe and
lunar travel are all housed below two of the largest telescopes in the
country. On a clear Friday or Saturday night you can go for free
and take a peak at Jupiter's storm with your own eyes. Don't miss
the planetarium; the immersive space show includes some of the
first pictures of the universe as a whole—it blew my mind.

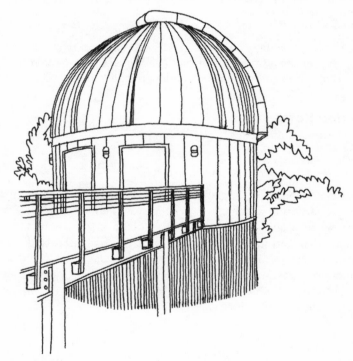

Chabot Observatory, Skyline Boulevard

East Bay Regional Parks

Further information about Huckleberry, Sibley, Botanical Gardens and Tilden:
2950 Peralta Oaks Court
562-PARK
www.ebparks.org

Huckleberry Botanic Regional Preserve

Atop the Oakland hills curves Huckleberry Trail, cutting through the small canyon ripples and passing through lush manzanita and madrone groves. At the start of the trail, off Skyline Boulevard, is a wooden box where you can pick up a self-guided tour map describing the area's flora and fauna. Lookout areas yield breathtaking views of the east and Mt. Diablo. The hike is a medium-grade loop, a good length for an afternoon stroll.

Sibley Volcanic Reserve

Further toward Berkeley from Huckleberry Trail is Sibley Volcanic Reserve. After all, the East Bay hills were not only formed by fault lines, but by volcanoes as well. Stay on the trail as you wind around forested bends and grassy knolls. It can be hard finding a loop that returns to the parking lot; I would suggest backtracking after you reach the labyrinth, located off a precipice at the end of the right branch of the trail going out from the parking lot.

Tilden Park

Around the staggering curves and bends at the top of the East Bay hills lies Tilden Park, perhaps most well known for its miniature railroad. It is a great spot for families to congregate, with the train for memorable rides and oodles of smiles, picnic grounds and horseback riding.

Tilden Park Botanic Garden

Located in Tilden Park, this botanic garden supports the vegetation of every county in the state. The climate is such that both alpine and desert, seaside and plains plants are all happy in this park. It is wondrous the variety of climate and native vegetation that covers the state of California, and this is a unique opportunity to see it all in one place. It has quite a romantic feel.

Oakland Walking Tours

Frank H. Ogawa Plaza, Broadway at 14th Street
238.3234
www.oaklandnet.com/walkingtours
Tours: W & Sat 10a

Choose from tours of Old Oakland, the City Center, Uptown and the Lake, Preservation Park, Chinatown, Jack London Waterfront, Churches and Temples, and New Era/New Politics. Discover the history, famous people and architecture of Oakland for free. Call to make a reservation, for the Wednesday and Saturday tours.

Western Aerospace Museum

8260 Boeing Street, North Field
www.westernaerospacemuseum.org
638-7100
Open: W-Sun 10a-4p (flying boat tours on Sundays)

Created by local aviation enthusiasts and historians, this museum remembers aviation greats Charles Lindberg and Amelia Earhart and the vintage planes and jets that have graced Oakland's skies. The 'Women in Aviation' exhibit is particularly well done.

Morcom Rose Garden

700 Jean Street at Grand Avenue
238-3187

During the late spring months the hills above Grand Avenue blossom with color. It is a friendly and welcoming garden where people of all ages come to enjoy the greenery and the perfumed air of roses. This garden is known as a popular spot for marriage proposals.

Dunsmuir House

2960 Peralta Oaks Court at Peralta Oaks Drive
615.5555
Open: Tu-F 10a-4p; tours W 11a
Admission: $5, free for children 13 and under

The 37-room Dunsmuir Mansion was built in 1878 by a wealthy coal baron from Canada. His house has seen all the ups and downs throughout the area's history and has become a recognizable landmark in Oakland. The entirety of the original 50-acre property has been restored as a historical site, educational space, and grounds for special occasions. The Tiffany style, neoclassical revival building is a truly gorgeous, and a wonderful place to lull about in the afternoon sun.

Peralta Hacienda

2465 34th Avenue at Salisbury Street
532.9142
info@peraltahacienda.org
Grounds open: M-F 9a-11p, house Tu-Th 4-530p

Peralta Hacienda Historical Park has been the eyes and ears of California's cultural cycles. The land has changed hands as Spaniards and Mexicans took over the native tribes, and the Eastern settlers assumed control. Check out this epic story in person at the estate.

Preservation Park

1233 Preservation Park Way at 13th Street
874.7580

Preservation Park is a testament to the civic abundance that Oakland was known for in the late 19th Century. Today this beautifully renovated collection of historic buildings offers a unique respite from the hustle and bustle of Oakland's city center. It is a perfectly romantic place for a picnic. Go to the White House across from the central fountain for a self-guided tour map of the homes.

USS Potomac

540 Water Street at Washington Street
627.1215
Open: M-Tu 9a-1p, W-F 9a-5p, Sat-Sun Noon-330p

President FDR's Floating White House has undergone a 12-year renovation that makes this vessel one of the finest examples of a World War II Navy ship. The military theme blends with presidential elegance where New Deal ideas were formulated to lift the US out of the Great Depression. Historical cruises and dock-side tours are available. Special events are held on major holidays.

Gondola Servizio

Lake Merritt Boating Center
568 Bellevue Avenue at Perkins Street
Open: Everyday 10a-Midnight
Fares start at $55

Gondola Servizio offers 55-minute cruises in authentic Venetian gondolas on Lake Merritt.

Heinold's First and Last Chance Saloon

48 Webster Street at Embarcadero West
839.6761
info@heinoldsfirstandlastchance.com
Open: M-F Noon-11p, M 3-10p, Sat-Sun 11a-10p

Continuously open since way back in 1883, Heinold's was passed down each generation in the same family until the mid 1980's. Famous as Jack London's favorite place to get sloshed, Heinhold's has the historical charm and the bay view that has continued to inspire customers for so many years. The original bar and stove remain intact, and most of the original whaling ship the bar was made from lives on, though the structure is now supported with newer material.

Camron-Stanford House

1418 Lakeside Drive at 14th Street
444.1876
Tours: 2nd and 3rd W, 11a & 4p, 3rd Sun 1 & 5p
Admission: $3-5

The Camron-Stanford House is the last of the private residences that were built around Lake Merritt in the 1870's. Home to some of the cities most famous families; it is now a Victorian museum, complete with a traditional teatime.

Cohen-Bray House

1440 29th Avenue at International Boulevard
563.1703
Open: 4th Sun 2p
Admission: Donation of $5 requested

Once a month, on the fourth Sunday, the Cohen-Bray House is open to public for tours of the exquisite antiques and Victorian furnishings hidden inside.

Rotary Nature Center and Japanese Gardens

Lakeside Park
666 Bellevue Drive at Grand Avenue
763.8409
www.gsbf-bonsai.org
Open: W-F 11a-3p, Sat 10a-4p, Sun Noon-4p

Next to the historic bird sanctuary on the banks of Lake Merritt is an immaculate collection of Bonsai, Suiseki (water stones) and traditional Japanese-style gardens.

Learn

Courses, classes and seminars or all sorts, and places to take on new challenges

Flexing your brain muscle is a great way to enhance a vacation, or a prolonged visit to a place. Classes are also a great way to meet locals. My grandmother was never bored; at the ripe old age of 82 she took Chinese language classes, having no background in it at all. She always inspired me to listen up, and see what I could learn.

Tilden Park Botanic Garden

Wildcat Canyon Road and South Park Drive in Tilden Regional Park
www.nativeplants.org

Spring courses in beautiful Tilden Park offer an opportunity to identify native plants, get up to snuff on butterflies and botany, and learn local geology. Explore the interconnectedness of all these environmental factors. The Oakland hills are actually volcanic, not just tectonic. Pick up some new gardening skills with hands-on demonstrations from knowledgeable and passionate instructors. Oakland's climate is one of the world's most versatile: it can sustain plant species from coastal regions and high altitude mountains.

Junior Naturalist Summer Day Camp at Don Edwards Preserve

Newark Slough Learning Center, Fremont, CA
792.0222
http://desfbay.fws.gov

Join in on a fun ecology summer camp in the park preserve for kids. Most programs last several weeks. Check their website for up to date information. Go to http://www.ecologycenter.org/. Then click an 'Env Ed' (Environmental Education Guide) for a full list of all the camps and resources in the Bay Area. The Ecology Center is a great resource in itself which offers classes, workshops and demonstrations throughout the year.

Studio One Art Classes

1428 Alice Street at 14th Street
597.5027
www.oaklandnet.com/parks

Studio One has one-time classes and studio time, as well as longer sessions where you can hone your artistic talents. They teach glass blowing, metal shop, painting and drawing, and photography plus yoga and meditation. All classes are reasonably priced, and are cheaper for current students and seniors. Go online to get more up-to-date information.

Rock Paper Scissors Collective

2278 Telegraph Avenue at 23rd Street
238.9171
www.rpscollective.com

The mentality here is that everyone has something to teach and something to learn. Artists and creators of all different mediums are offered the space to teach and to take classes, free of charge, and in most cases, equipment is included. (See **Create** chapter for more information.)

Monart Fine Art Classes

1918 Encinal Avenue at Lafayette Street, Alameda
521.3729
http://alameda.monart.com

Get in touch with your creative side by learning the Monart drawing technique, known for connecting your vision with accurate and confident skills. All ages are welcome. The basis of many art forms is being able to draw, or see with your hands—these classes can provide you with a stable foundation.

Knitting Classes

Both Article Pract and The Knitting Basket host several knitting classes, from complete walkthroughs on specific projects, to free 15-minute help sessions. Vacation time is a great time to challenge yourself with some handwork, whether you are a beginner or a veteran. Take it on—there is support for you in Oakland. (See **Create** chapter for more information.)

Beading and Metal Works Classes

1676 Shattuck Avenue at Virginia Street, Berkeley
644.BEAD
www.baublesandbeads.com

Baubles and Beads has local metal workers and bead artists come in to teach in their well-equipped studio. Wow your friends when they compliment your new earrings by telling them you made them! (See **Create** chapter for more information.)

Sewing Classes at Stone Mountain and Daughter
2518 Shattuck Avenue at Dwight Way, Berkeley
845.6106
www.stonemountainfabric.com

One of the best fabric stores in town also hosts the best sewing classes. Learn to use a pattern, or work on a quilt or interior design project. Make your own sloper or a fitted suit jacket. The teachers are helpful and make you feel totally capable. Current class schedules are posted on their website.

Iaido Classes
Nishi Kaigan Iaido Dojo
231.0678
www.iaido.org
Classes in Oakland and San Francisco

Try your hand at this ancient slow-paced form of martial arts that focuses on strength and balance by using heavy wooden swords.

Capoeira Classes
Capoeira Arts Café
2026 Addison Street at Milvia Street, Berkeley
666.1255
www.capoeirarts.com

This traditional Brazilian dance/martial art is a lot of fun and gives you a great work out. Most of the teachers at Capoeira Arts Café have grown up with this art form, and share their passion and skills at classes from morning to night. Professional performers often show up on weekends, so you can hone your skills with drummers and other dancers. Check for up-to-date schedules on their website.

Free Dance Classes

Ashkenaz Music and Dance Community Center
1317 San Pablo Avenue at Gilman Street, Berkeley
Showline: 525.5054

The lessons usually start at 8:30, before the band arrives. The type of dance varies as widely as the types of music Ashkenaz attracts to its stage. You could be learning Rumba, Nigerian prayer formations or line dancing. Be ready to get down. On breaks you can sample vegetarian food and sip on a local microbrew.

Oakland Asian Cultural Center

388 9th Street at Franklin Street, Suite 290
637.0455
www.oacc.cc

Classes in everything from Chinese Operatic Technique to Break Dancing are offered in the heart of Chinatown. This inclusive place attracts an open-minded, talented crowd and highly skilled teachers. Classes are affordable and schedules on-going. Check out their main office on the top floor of Chinatown's mall, where you can ask questions and pick up the most up-to-date information.

Music Lessons

Oakland Public Conservatory of Music
1616 Franklin Street at 17th Street
836.4649
www.opcmusic.org

Voice and violin, percussion and piano, any and all other instruments can be learned through Oakland's organization of professional music teachers. Whatever genre or instrument you want to start or enhance your skill with, you can find a class to fit your needs. Private lessons are often taken in combination with ensemble workshops to build on both solo and group performances. Concert opportunities and musical partnerships abound.

Red Cross Health and Safety Classes

www.oaklandnet.com/parks

Be a more involved community citizen by taking a class in first aid or community safety. There are rotating schedules throughout the year through the city's parks and recreation department; they even have free classes once a year. Check the website for current course offerings.

Swimming Lessons

www.oaklandswimming.org

The Oakland Community Pool Project oversees the Undercurrents, the most diverse swim team in the world. To foster the team's growth, as well as bring the sport to downtown Oakland, they also have a swim school for all ages and abilities. Classes are offered year round at Laney College pool.

Kayaking 101

www.oaklandnet.com/parks

Spend a few hours kayaking on Lake Merritt for less than 20 dollars. You and your friends and family can receive the boat rental and a half an hour instruction in beginner kayaking. It is not often you get the chance to kayak through a city.

Peralta Community Colleges

www.peralta.cc.ca.us

The Peralta Colleges are some of the oldest in the state. They are funded by a collective of trusts set up by a community-oriented family who wanted to ensure that higher education be a viable option for anyone. There are several campuses: Laney, Alameda, Merritt and Vista. Many of the teachers also work at UC Berkeley, Mills or the California College of Arts and Crafts. The arts and technology classes are especially good.

Get Active

Hikes, runs, rides, bikes, boats– anything and everything to get you moving

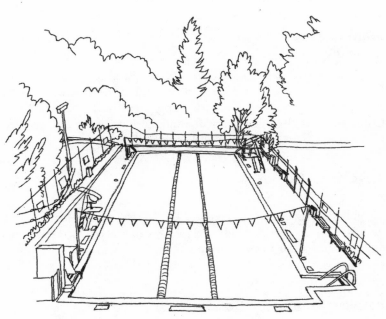

Lions Pool, Dimond Park

Lions Pool

Dimond Park, at the end of Wellington Street
482.7852
www.oaklandnet.com/parks/facilities/publicpools.asp
Open: Everyday 11a-230p, Tu-F 630-930a, M-Th 6-8p

Near Fruitvale and MacArthur, a finger of the lush Oakland hills dips into the city. Dimond Creek, and the surrounding Dimond Park make a lovely oasis for an afternoon stroll. There is a trail that goes up into the canyon, open space for picnics and several play structures, complete with the bounce-back foam flooring to cushion any potential falls. But the best part is Lions pool, heated to 82 degrees F year round and plopped right in the center of this green belt. Lap swim is open year round, three times a day, and recreational swim, youth swim team and lessons go from early June through August. It is not only the nicest outdoor pool in Oakland, and probably the warmest, but also the cheapest. Adults are 3 dollars; seniors 2.25 and you can save even more with a ten-pass card. The regulars that swim here are wonderful to talk to, and always have good tips on concerts and restaurants. It is a great place to meet locals and have a relaxing swim in a beautiful location. Lion's pool was opened as a gift to Oakland's children in 1927 by the Lions club. The City of Oakland parks and recreation department now operates it. Take Park Boulevard to Wellington Street, which dead ends at Dimond's parking lot. It's an easy walk from the Fruitvale and MacArthur bus stop.

Temescal Pool

371 45th Street at Lawton Avenue
597.5013
www.oaklandnet.com/parks/facilities/publicpools.asp
Open: M-F 630-845a, 1230-230p & 5-7p, Sat-Sun 11a-230p

A cooler pool than Lions, Temescal has the get-down-to-business lap swimmer crowd down pat. The same punch pass at Lions works here.

Roberts Recreation Area

Off Skyline Boulevard towards Chabot Space and Science Center
info@ebparks.org
544.2210

The park's facilities include a swimming pool, archery range, hiking trails, ball fields and stables. Have a picnic at one of the outlook points and you'll be sandwiched between the redwoods and a breath taking view.

Wheels of Justice

2024 Mountain Boulevard at La Salle Avenue
339.6091
www.wojcyclery.com
Open: M-Sat 11a-6p, Sun 11a-5p

Wheels of Justice offers rental bikes and mopeds, plus affordable bikes with lifetime warranties. They have superb service. It's also probably the best place in the East Bay for a tune-up.

Bay Area Bikes

1050 West Grand Avenue at Linden Street
763.BIKE
www.bayareabikes.com
Open: M-F 11a-7p, Sat 10a-6p, Sun 11a-5p

The friendliest bike store in town, Bay Area Bikes carries top of the line bikes and equipment.

Hank and Frank

6030 College Avenue at Chabot Road
654.2453
www.hankandfrankbicycles.com
Open: M-Sat 10a-6p, Sun 11a-5p

These guys are the mountain bike and BMX specialists of the Bay Area.

Montclair Sports

1970 Mountain Boulevard at La Salle Avenue
339.9313
Open: M-W & F-Sat 930a-6p, Th 930a-8p, Sun 10a-5p

A family business since the 1950's, this place stocks equipment for all types of sports, and if they don't have it in store, they'll order it for you. Check out their great selection of swim gear.

See Jane Run

5817 College Avenue at Oak Grove Avenue
428.2681
www.seejanerunsports.com
Open: M-F 11a-7p, Sat 10a-6p, Sun 11a-6p

Finally there is store catering to women athletes, where you can find clothes and equipment that fits right. They also organize women's training teams, and are full of helpful tips and suggestions, whatever your sport of level. The place just has good vibes, and even though a lot of the inventory is pretty styling, the emphasis is on cultivating a love of movement, and not the fashion-show gym mentality that plagues so many sport shops.

Cleveland Cascade, Lakeshore Avenue

Lake Merritt Trail and Cleveland Cascade

Along Grand Avenue and Lakeshore Boulevard
www.oaklandnet.com/parks/parks/lakemerritt.asp
www.clevelandcascade.org

A 3-mile run and a multi-tiered outdoor staircase (between 2250 & 2300 Lakeshore Boulevard)are great for really working up a sweat, or take a leisurely stroll, whatever suits your mood. This is where Reggie Jackson used to run during his tenure with the Oakland A's. I think it is safe to say everyone here in Oakland has a soft spot for Lake Merritt; it is the heart of the city.

Park Boulevard Yoga

4226 Park Boulevard at Glenfield Avenue
798.3712
www.parkyoga.com
Class schedules vary

Park Boulevard Yoga is a holistic yoga studio that focuses on asana postures with top teachers. The morning classes are a wonderful way to start out your day on the right foot.

Oakland Ice Center

519 18th Street at Broadway
268.9000
www.oaklandice.com
Open: MWF Noon-4p, F 7-10p, Tu-Th Noon-5p, 7-830p,
Sat-Sun 130-5p. 7-10p

Hockey and figure skating classes, plus free-skate sessions and lessons, Oakland Ice Center covers everything relating to ice rinks.

Buy Me

A unique take on shopping from artichokes to zippers

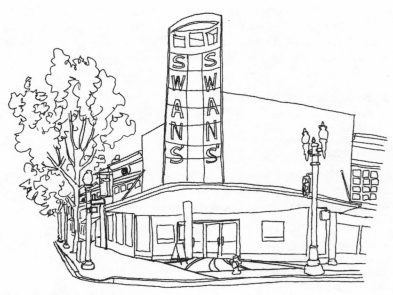

Swan's Market, Washington Street

Andy Warhol really had something when he equated department stores with museums. Indeed, the way that to appeal to shoppers is an artful task, and well represents are most modern takes on design and cultural signing. So whether you have a practical purpose, need a little retail therapy or just want to gaze around at the most modern of museums, these spots should fulfill your aims, while also being community and environment-friendly businesses.

Swan's Market

901 Washington Street at 9th Street
www.swansmarket.com

Historically this was the local market where housewives would go to get their daily produce and meat. There still remains gracious meat vendors and several small fish stands, but the market has branched out to bath supplies, a florist, several restaurants, cheeses, and vegetable. Get a smoothie and sip away while you pick up barbeque provisions. Make sure to check out the beautiful tile work around the block-long structure, and the kid's art museum (MOCHA) next door. Note the garden around the corner–it is part of a successful inner-city co-housing community.

Neldam's Danish Bakery

3401 Telegraph Avenue at 34th Street
658.1967
www.neldamsbakery.com
Open: M-F 7a-6p, Sat 8a-5p, Sun 10a-3p

Opened in 1928, Neldam's has been baking pure yumminess for four generations. They make outstanding cardamom bread, croissants, and strawberry cake. This is the place to get classic cakes and cookies, made from scratch. Don't expect whole wheat or organic ingredients, Neldam's is a traditional bakery and hasn't gotten into the whole California cuisine thing. But they do use fresh whipped cream in their outstanding strawberry cake, and house-made marzipan in some of the Danishes and cookies. I once had a cake shipped to me from Neldam's for my birthday, and I haven't missed a year since. Go to their website to get the password for the monthly special, there is always a great deal on something sweet.

Cultural Crossroads

3223 Grand Avenue at Lake Park Avenue
663.2374
www.shopculturalcrossroads.com
Open: Tu-F 11a-5p, Sat 10a-6p

Ethnic clothes and home décor to spruce up anyone's living space are just starters here. This local business is actively involved with several community initiatives, including working with people re-entering the workforce. There always seems to be some sale going on, whether it is patchwork halter-tops or filigree rings, tasseled throw pillows or beaded slippers.

Entrez! Open House

1645 Telegraph Avenue at 17th Street
268.9101
www.influencesbymarie.com
Open: M-Th 10a-6p, F-Sat 11a-7p

This new local business brings European design to Oakland's City Center. A German dish scrubber with an Afro, Swedish glassware, Italian lamps, elegant coffee tables and hilarious sticky notes and gifts—Entrez! completes the worldliness of this city with a sweet and colorful charm. Monthly Happy Hour gatherings, co-hosted by next-door Café Azusa feature pleasant music and refreshing drinks.

Walden Pond Books

3316 Grand Avenue at Elwood Avenue
832.4438
www.waldenpondbooks.com
Open: Sun-Th 10a-9p, F-Sat 10a-10p

Privately owned since it's opening in 1973, you can find a wide variety of titles, from Japanese gardening to the history of the Lakota tribe. Their rare books are catalogued online. The friendly knowledgeable staff can always help you in your search. They offer student and teacher discounts.

The Meadows

6307 College Avenue at 6rd Street
653.3322
Open: Everyday 7a-8p

The Meadows is the best flower store in Oakland. Their flowers are the freshest, most beautiful and longest lasting I have found, and trust me, I've searched. Next to breathing and a few other things, flowers are a necessity to me. I once bought lilies here that lasted into the third week, and when some hydrangeas faded fast they were replaced free of charge.

Pimlico Place

4135 Piedmont Avenue at 41st Street
655.7081
Open: M-Sat 11a-7p, Sun 11a-5p
(Annex shop closed Mondays)

This place is a playground of color. From tea sets to cool jewelry, you walk into a wonderland of delightful things. Come here for your throw pillows made from all sorts of fabrics in different styles and sizes. One sister owns this business, the other helps out working in the annex shop right around the corner.

Maribel

3251 Lakeshore Avenue at Lake Park Avenue
419.0677
Open: M-Sat 10a-6p, Sun 11a-5p,
Consignment M-Sat 10a-2p

Maribel is a great meeting place of quality used clothes and funky wear by new designers. Each item is picked with a keen eye on style and cut. Most of the pieces are unique, or take on a new incarnation of a traditional style. Pick up your party outfit, or film premier clothes, or even a classy winter coat. If you are into lots of color, this is the place for you. There is a sale rack in the back where impressive discounts can often be hunted down. Reusing clothes and fabrics is an important aspect of living an environmentally sound life, but it doesn't mean you can't look gorgeous!

Montclair Wines

6140 Medau Place at Mountain Boulevard
339.8405
www.montclairwines.com
Open: M-F 1030a-7p, Sat 10a-6p, Sun 11a-5p

I was always taught that as a guest I should show up with something in my hands, just as a gesture. A nice wine makes a great housewarming gift, or party addition, and really shows genuine gratitude. Why schlep a heavy vintage on an airplane when you can find numerous international wines in Montclair? These guys truly know their stuff. They carry rare spirits and micro-brews too, plus non-alcoholic beers. It has been owned and operated by the same group of connoisseurs for some time.

Heartfelt

6309 College Avenue at 63rd Street
655.9806
www.heartfeltsf.com
Open: M-Sat 10a-7p, Sun 10a-5p

From twinkling cherry blossom branches to beautiful hand made soaps, owner Darcy Lee sells interesting treasures made by designers and artists with an innovative flare. The jewelry, cards, and pillows have a practical purpose, together with personality and a sense of humor. I especially like the collection of creative key chains and miniature sculptures.

Pendragon Books

5560 College Avenue at Ocean View Drive
652.6259
www.pegasusbookstore.com
Open: M-Sat 10a-1045p, Sun 10a-9p

Few booksellers can say they have been able to stay independent for over 30 years. Pendragon can. By my thinking, their commitment to quality books and hard to find magazines, plus local, independent publishers and authors has given them true staying power. Come here to discover a new British magazine, or an underground 'zine', a beautifully photographed cookbook, or the latest 'employee-pick' novel. They will also buy or trade for your old books and CDs.

Sagrada Sacred Arts

4926 Telegraph Avenue at 49th Street
653.7196
www.sagrada.com
Open: Tu-Sat 10a-5p

I love the movie Chocolat. At the end of the movie, there is a line about being defined "by what you embrace and not what you exclude." Sagrada has a similar message, embracing the diversity of faiths in the world, and bringing them together in one respectful space. There are books and religious objects from Christianity, Judaism, Buddhism and Islam all stacked on the same shelves. Mutual understanding and communication is key to peace. There is also a great children's section, so kids can start on their own spiritual path, wherever it may lead.

Diesel, A Bookstore

5433 College Avenue at Kales Avenue
653.9965
http://diesel.booksense.com
Open: M-Th 10a-9p, F-Sat 10a-10p, Sun 10a-6p

Diesel is more than a bookstore. Monthly Spanish-speaking nights and fun outings to local restaurants are part of a continual calendar that brings the pursuit of knowledge to life. Books are handpicked, and employees are familiar with most of the stores titles. Author signings are a regular occurrence. Check the front counter for outstanding new titles.

Piedmont Lane Antiques

4121 Piedmont Avenue at 41st Street
654.4706
Open: M-Sat 11a-6p

For the collector in all of us there is Piedmont Lane, a series of rooms and storefronts filled with all things collectable. From vintage aprons and Bakelite bracelets to 19th Century Japanese woodblock prints and handcrafted furniture, the seemingly endless set of rooms are toppling full.

Le Bonbon

2050 Mountain Boulevard at La Salle Avenue
339.2962
Open: Everyday 10a-6p

Few gifts top chocolate, and few chocolates top Mozart, the Austrian specialty truffle available here. For those of you who haven't yet experienced this bliss, it is a dark chocolate covered, pistachio cream wafer truffle sort of thing; really it belies explanation. Le Bonbon is one of the few places where you can buy the real deal as there are many Mozart impostors. Godiva chocolates, Jelly Belly beans, fragrant teas and other gifts are always in stock.

Keeping Kosher in Oakland:

There are many stores and restaurants across the city that have Kosher supervision Beth Jacob Orthodox synagogue (www.bethjacoboakland.org) has a complete listing of Kosher supervised places around the Bay Area on their website. Grand Bakery and Oakland Kosher Foods are supervised by Va'ad Ha Kashrus of Northern California (415.543.0900) and Holy Land, (see **Do Lunch** chapter), is strictly supervised by Beth Jacob Rabbi Judah Dardik.

Oakland Kosher Foods

3419 Lakeshore Avenue at Mandana Boulevard
839.0177
Open: M-F 9a-p5, closed: Saturdays and Jewish Holidays

Have you ever tried Israeli delicacies? My favorite is leben, a yogurt-like pudding that just melts in your mouth. Oakland Kosher Foods stocks many Israeli and Far East treats, interesting cookies, snacks, great salads, and kosher meat. This store is family owned, by locals who wanted to bring quality kosher food and authentic Israeli delights to the Oakland community.

Grand Bakery (Kosher)

3264 Grand Avenue at Lake Park Avenue
465.1110
Open: Tu-F 8a-4p, closed: Mondays, Saturdays and Jewish Holidays

Ever played name that tune with the local baker? Well then head over to Grand Bakery, my favorite place to get oven-fresh cookies and hear a good joke. On my last visit the guy next in line was given a free poppy seed hamantaschen for knowing the name of a Who song. They make bread and both sweet and savory treats. This is one lively kitchen, and a family business to boot.

Shopping Districts

Old Oakland

Newly restructured, with further development and sidewalk repavement planned in the near future, Old Oakland is getting back the Victorian charm it had at the turn of the last century. New stylish clubs and restaurants are popping up. Swan's Market and Mexicali Rose are still local fixtures. Old Oakland is blooming, and is, hands down, my favorite place to stroll around in the whole city.

Jack London Square

Jack London Square has an internationally inspired shopping scene. You can buy everything from a genuine African woven bag to a French beret. Go on Sundays for the weekly craft fair and farmers market, which usually features a live band (see **Weekend** chapter). If you have the energy, stay for a night out at Kimball's, Yoshi's, the Metro, or one of the many nightclubs around the corner.

Chinatown

This lively part of Oakland's City Center is certainly not limited to Chinese stores and restaurants. Cambodian, Filipino, Vietnamese, Korean, Japanese and Thai people also own businesses here, which makes it such a unique place. The open markets and countless small eateries provide endless adventure.

Montclair

The posh hills of Montclair don't carry the snobby attitude of some other wealthy city areas. Stores along the curvy hills are mostly locally owned. This is a close-knit community, but the people here don't ever make you feel like an outsider. Montclair Village has the most condensed shopping area of any in Oakland, and has a lovely little park, too.

Grand Avenue and Lakeshore Boulevard

These two parallel streets are home to some wonderful Oakland shops. A happy mixture of cafés, music stores, bakeries, bookstores, and boutiques, there is something for everyone. Walden Pond Books on Grand is a highlight, also the kosher bakery a few doors down. Holy Land Israeli restaurant is nestled between these two streets, and serves some outstanding Israeli lemonade, perfect to re-hydrate on a break from shopping.

Piedmont Avenue

Piedmont Avenue is not only home to some of the top Oakland restaurants, but also some wonderful boutiques and stores. Unique art galleries and local bookstores line this rather upscale street. It is a great place to find things uniquely Oakland; you won't find any chain stores here. Go to peruse the shops then grab a bite at one of the great restaurants, then a movie at the independent Piedmont Theater.

Temescal

The up-and-coming Temescal district is home to some of the best restaurants and shops in the city. Stroll along the northern part of Telegraph past bakeries, belly dancing studios, pizzerias, and artful home décor shops. Temescal is to Oakland what Soho was to New York in the early 90's.

College Avenue, Rockridge

Rockridge is very posh. There is a small town feel to the interesting shops that run over two miles of College Avenue. There's a gourmet food mall, a women's sports specialty store, handmade kids clothes and toy stores, several bookstores, an eyeglass store, clothing stores, and restaurants. College Avenue is a wonderful alternative to mega stores.

Fruitvale

A colorful selection of stores, large and small, are clustered around the Fruitvale BART station. Fruitvale is the heart of the Spanish-speaking community. Here you can find the best Mexican food in the city, plus some great thrift stores and handmade craft vendors.

Laurel

This area is a mixture of great diners, small bookstores, beauty supply stores and an organic farmer's market. It is a richly diverse area that and offers a hilltop view of the bay like no other shopping area.

Crowds

Major league sports, international celebrations, and other exciting sardine cans

Here's a listing of my favorite crowded places:

The White Horse Inn

6551 Telegraph Avenue at 65th Street
652.3820
Open: M-Tu 3p-2a, W-Sun 1p-2a

The oldest gay bar in California is now a local haunt for every gender and sexual orientation. With a fireplace, great theme nights, big screen TV's, video games and no room for quick judgments, this is one of the most fun places to go at night in Oakland. Come before 9pm to get in for free, or on Thursdays with you college ID.

The Alley

3325 Grand Avenue at Elwood Avenue
444.8505
Open: Everyday 5p-midnight

This classic neighborhood piano bar is an old-time alternative to karaoke. Rod Dibble plays nightly music, requested and accompanied by the audience composed largely of regulars. In the center of this interior decorator's conundrum sits the bar, attached to the vintage piano. Nightgowns hang from the walls, that is, where the business cards aren't taking over. Go for a cheap and tasty steak dinner before a round of singing, served until 10pm. This is Oakland at its friendliest.

Athletics Baseball at the Oakland Coliseum

Coliseum Way at 65th Street
762.2255
www.oaklandathletics.com
www.tickets.com

Tickets: $7-32, $2 on Wednesdays. Buy them at the box office, over the phone, or online. The Coliseum is conveniently connected to BART. Parking at the Coliseum is $14.

Raiders at the Oakland Coliseum

762.2277
www.raidernation.com

Tickets: $47-91 and frequently sell out early.

Warriors at the Arena in Oakland

888.479.4667
www.warriors.com

Tickets range from $10 to $270, and are available at the box office, by phone, or through Ticketmaster.

Golden Gate Fields Racetrack

1100 Eastshore Highway at the Gilman Street off-ramp of Interstate 80/580, Albany
559.7300
www.ggfields.com
Open: W-Sun

Thoroughbred racing with some of the country's best jockeys and horses is right here on the lip of the East Bay. Racing season runs from November through early May.

Stay Up Late

Where to find midnight snacks, 24-hour businesses and casual late night drinking, dining and dancing

Legendary Palace, Franklin Street

Staying up late to dance and dine and relax is something everyone does at least once in a while, so here are the best places around to get in touch with your nocturnal side.

Legendary Palace

708 Franklin Street at 7th Street
663.9188
Open: M-F 9a-330p, 5p-Midnight, Sat-Sun 8a-Midnight

If you're hungry on a late night in Chinatown the pickins' are slim. The commotion of the daytime market is wrapped up and most of the restaurants shut their doors by the time darkness sets in. But wouldn't you know it, one of the better dim sum places is open 'til midnight 7 days a week, and they have free parking to boot, unheard of in the bustling trafficked Chinatown streets. Legendary Palace is hard to miss. From the outside it seems like a tourist trap, decked out with red lanterns and tacky Chinese temple trappings. Large cut glass chandeliers hover over nearly every table. But don't judge this book by its cover. This is where all of Chinatown eats, but conveniently not all at the same time, the place is never as crowded as Jade Villa, around the corner. The authentic dim sum plates are first class. Since few of the servers speak enough English to explain what the dishes are, I would encourage a little experimentation. Most of the things you may not be accustomed to eating look like what they are-the boiled chicken feet look like, well, boiled chicken feet. The stewed baby octopi are colored red, from the sauce, but are still very noticeable. The dumplings and noodle rolls are usually filled with pork.

Lanesplitter Pizza

4799 Telegraph Avenue at 46th Street
653.5350
www.lanesplitterpizza.com

You can debate about which is better, the deep dish or the crispy thin crust, in this pumped up pizzeria until 130 in the morning. Order any beer before 6 and it is a dollar off. Order a salad and you get a hearty bowl enough to feed you and all your friends. Loud music goes well with zesty bread sticks and the motorcycle motif.

House of Chicken and Waffles

444 Embarcadero West at Broadway
836.4446
Open: Sun-Th 8a-Midnight, F-Sat 8a-4a

Sometimes when you are up too late your vision starts to go blurry, and small print menus challenge your nocturnal glow. Luckily, House of Chicken and Waffles thought of that, and painted the menu in bright colors on the wall, so you can just point and they will bring you gigantic portions of delicious hot food. Smooth grits, fluffy waffles, maple sweet potatoes, and the best fried chicken around are waiting to fill your belly. I feel a wave of comfort come on as soon as I enter the place. Don't miss the cheese gracious omelet or the honey sweetened yams; they are beyond satisfying.

Kimball's Carnival

522 2nd Street at Embarcadero West
444.6979
www.kimballscarnival.com
Open: M-Sat 11a-Midnight, F-Sat 8p-2a

When you are feeling a bit more well-to-do, check out Kimball's where great dancing and fancy drinks mingle with an energetic atmosphere. Go on Wednesdays when they have free salsa or swing classes before the live band picks up.

The Stork Club

2330 Telegraph Avenue at 23rd Street
444.6174
Open: Tu-W & Sun 4p-2a, F-Sat 1p-2a (happy hour 4p-7p)

For an intimate experience with hard rock, head over to the Stork. There are usually two bands each night, the softer of the two performing first. Listen to improv jazz or heavy metal while you sip reasonably priced drinks and brush up on your pool skills. Don't let the funky décor fool you; these digs are privy to some pretty sensational sounds.

Mexicali Rose

701 Clay Street at 7th Street
451.2450
Open: Everyday 11a-1a

Mexicali Rose is open until 130 am every day of the week. They serve huge portions of no-frills Mexican cuisine, as well as 13 different tequilas. The chicken tacos are the best, fresh-made tortillas with well-stewed and flavorful chicken, pressed into a cute and easy-to-eat scallop shape and heaping with lettuce and pico de gallo. The wet enchiladas are also a star. I need a to-go box even when I split a plate with my honey. Everything is reasonably priced, and the atmosphere is fun. The same family has owned and operated this business for 71 years, moving across the street once; some of the cooks have been re-frying beans in Rose's kitchen for 30 years.

Pamper

Shelters from the hustle and bustle, simple enjoyments, and all things feel-good

Part of the whole pampering process is good, hot, comfort food. The classic is chicken soup. But I find most places load their chicken broth up with salt, as a substitute for slow-cooked flavor. This is bad news for the body; instead of pampering you get seriously dehydrated. So in this chapter I've given special attention to not only the in-the-moment effects, but the after effects as well. Here is a selection of feel-good foods, restful spaces and of course, spas and salons to refresh, re-energize, and restart your engines.

Michael Mischer Chocolates

3352 Grand Avenue at Mandana Boulevard
986.1822
www.michaelmischerchocolates.com
Open: Everyday Noon-9pm

Chocolate is one of the best things to get me back on the right track. And what could be better than fine chocolates, European gelato and top-notch espresso all in one place? Michael Mischer's handcrafted treats are a mini vacation in and of themselves. There are chocolate bars with candied orange peel and espresso beans, pear brandy truffles, and the best gelato I've had outside of Germany. Try a combination of Madagascar vanilla and giarunda (chocolate and hazelnut) for a truly blissful moment. The man himself is often in the store, having owned and operated his own Grand Avenue location since 2004. Anyone who wants to go to Europe, or wants to reminisce about his or her last trip there will especially enjoy this place.

Sweet Adeline Bakeshop

3350 Adeline Street at 63rd Street
985.7381
www.sweetadelinebakeshop.com
Open: M-Sat 7a-6p, Sun 8a-5p
$ Fr S Vtn

Sweet Adeline is a cozy and comfortable bakery. Cake stands are cluttered with rhubarb muffins, ganache confections, toasty breads and fruity galettes. This is one of the few places where there is little disagreement—Sweet Adeline makes this otherwise barren stretch of Adeline Street, well... sweet! The prices are reasonable, the service is friendly, the treats are astounding and they have renovated the space to be a perfect nook for chewing and chumming, or reading and relaxing.

XOX Truffles

6126 La Salle Avenue at Mountain Boulevard
3399.XOX
www.xoxtruffles.com
Open: M-Sat 9a-7p, Sun 9a-4p

XOX is one of the fine chocolate makers that give the Bay Area a worldly renown for cocoa confections. Each handmade truffle is dusted in raw cacao powder. Essences are blended with the strong and creamy dark chocolate, with no over-sugared butter cream filling. Come in for a coffee or any of their soothing hot drinks and get a truffle on the house. Red Wine, Cognac and Hazelnut are the best flavors.

Lulu Rae Confections

6311 College Avenue at 63rd Street
54.Sweet
www.lulurae.com
Open: M-Th 9a-8p, F-Sat 9a-9p, Sun 9a-7p

Owner Shelly Grubb, picks her favorite chocolates and sweets from around the world and gathers them neatly on glass shelves of temptation. Godiva, XOX, Schaffen Berger and German, Swiss and Belgian makers sit daintily beside house-made confections and a case of creamy gelato. The spicy Mayan hot chocolate can't be beat.

Nola's Skin Care Boutique

3231 Grand Avenue at Santa Clara Avenue
451.0271
Open: Tu-F 11a-7p, Sat 10a-6p, Sun 10a-5p

Independent and locally owned, Nola's is a charming place to smooth out your frazzled self. The staff are as courteous as ever, circulating around you in the most complete way, alike to a fairy godmother. This is a far-cry from the clandestine office worker setting that I have seen at other skin care salons, where scheduling seems to be a bigger priority than a moment of bliss.

The Nail Shop

3326 Grand Avenue at Mandana Boulevard
832.6245
Open: Everyday 10a-7p

Choosing among one of the million nail salons on Grand Avenue can be tricky. Some have sub-par cleanliness; others are fantastic and carry heavy price tags. The Nail Shop is a favorite choice because it charges somewhere in the middle, and can be trusted give a superior mani- or pedicure. The only problem is that most Oaklanders with a penchant for getting their nails done know about this place. There are always people here, or people waiting, even men. It is for good reason.

Au Natural

2071 Antioch Court, Suite 200 at Mountain Boulevard
339.1152
Open: Tu-F 10a-7p, Sat 8a-4p

A skin rejuvenation center au natural, the fully licensed and certified caregivers will doll you up with the most luxurious of nature's products. They also do impeccable waxing jobs and organic facials that take you straight to cloud nine.

Nailphoria

1212 Broadway Suite 910 (9th Floor) at 9th Street
893.2181
www.nailphoria.com
Open: M-F 10a-7p, Sat 9a-6p

Another family run business is making quite a name for itself for the best manicure around. They can no longer accommodate drop-ins. Luckily appointments are readily available and easy to schedule by calling in and speaking with one of the talented ladies. Try a new color of polish and relax your feet with a salt scrub and soak.

Pho Hoa Lao

720 International Boulevard at East 22nd Avenue
451.6888
Open: Everyday 8a-8p
$ Fr Fam

Vietnamese soup seriously rivals America's traditional chicken noodle. A big bowl of somewhat sweet pho broth with all kinds of meaty morsels warms you from the inside out, calming your nerves. I like Pho Hoa Lao the most because it is a large, more relaxed space, with long tables meant for the whole family to join in on slurping and sipping. It also specializes in pho (the pronunciation of which I have yet to master, despite innumerable sincere attempts), and doesn't try to cram in sweet and sour pork and the Americanized Asian dishes so many other pho places do. The broth is translucent, I am told a very good sign of the authentic, slow-cooked technique. Go out on a limb and try the *dak biet*, or house special, that includes a variety of meats. Or if you only want flank you can specify, but the type of meat is really the only difference down the pho menu. Each huge bowl is served with fresh greens, bean sprouts, lemon and sauces. For the best results, put the bean sprouts in right away so they cook a bit; stir them with the rare meat and both will be fully cooked through by the time you take your first slurp. I was taught to mix the hoisin sauce and the wonderful vermillion *sriracha* sauce for dipping the meat chunks, and when the noodles and meat were all finished, to squeeze the lemon in the broth and sip away. I can split one order and be full without seeing the bowl's bottom.

Stay In

The best take out, and take-home activities in town

Sometimes I try and pack too much into a day. By evening, all systems are not go. But taking in the town can be done inside too. There are many great restaurants that specialize in to-go food, or places where the seating isn't as comfortable, so you can choose one of these low-energy nights to have an in-hotel or in-home dinner. While you're at it why not rent a flick, or even one of the many movies made here in Oaktown.

Zza's Trattoria
552 Grand Avenue at Euclid Avenue
839.9124
www.zzasrestaurant.com
Open: Tu-Sun 11a-3p, Sun-Th 5-10p, F-Sat 5-11p
$$ Fam S Vtn

Finally, a simple yet authentic Italian restaurant has decided to offer free delivery service. Imagine having al dente pastas, perfectly seasoned, not wearing an enormous price tag, brought right to your door. Try their chicken and rosemary rotelle, barley soup with wild mushrooms and prosciutto, or a calzone stuffed with smoked chicken breast and cilantro pesto.

Gregoire
4001B Piedmont Avenue at MacArthur Boulevard
547.3444
www.gregoirerestaurant.com
Open: Everyday 11a-9p
$$ Ro Vtn

The most authentic French cooking in Oakland is take out! Gregoire is a Frenchman in every respect, cooking at an open stove while chatting away in French, or with his identifiable accent. The fruits of his labor are melt-in-your mouth potatoes, poached fish, and divine meat dishes, not to mention delicious soups and salads. The leek lentil is supernal, and healthy, and the truffle dressing he puts on organic frisée is a whole new level for salad. You can sit on the few bar stools for lunch, but all the food is designed for take away, packed neatly into elegant hexagonal boxes made from recycled post-consumer content. Gregoire's is a little bit of France, hidden away in Oakland.

Global Entertainment
5132 Telegraph Avenue at 51st Street
428.0707
Open: Everyday 10a-11p

Choose from 17 thousand movie titles under one roof. Global's comprehensive selection includes two copies of all of Keislowski's Decalogues, hard to find documentaries and an entire section of independent films, in the front, no less. It is easy even for travelers to rent films, you just need some kind of bankcard, and a name, of course. Most films are 5-day rentals, and cost about 3 bucks. A couple gripes: the foreign section actually means non-English language films, so Irish, British, and other English language foreign titles are mixed throughout the rest of the huge room. The films are all alphabetized in categories by title, not by director or any other means of organization. The computer system can help with finding that film, you know, that film with what's his name in it... (PS: Please check out Kieslowski's films if you haven't all ready!)

Purple Pepper Pizza

5335 College Avenue at Manila Avenue
653.5001
www.purplepepperpizza.com
Open: Sun-Th 10-11, F-Sat 10-12
$ Fam Vtn

The tastiest, best value for delivery pizza in Oakland is Purple Pepper. They use the right amount of cheese, quality toppings and a medium thick crust–a compromise for the deep dish versus thin and crispy debate. The delivery is fast and they have an excellent track record for getting the orders right the first time. Try the Rockridgian with ricotta for a creamier alternative to plain mozzarella. The Kitchen Sink is covered with meat of every sort, making it the most decadent pizza around.

The Cuckoo's Nest

247 4th Street at Jefferson Street
452.9414
Open: M-W 8a-730p, Th-F 8a-9p, Sat-Sun 8a-2p
$$ Fam Vtn

Cuckoo's Nest serves traditional menu items in a larger-than-life way. I ordered a turkey sandwich to go and got a giant, grilled Acme French roll, with steamy cuts of fresh turkey, stuffed with Dijon and organic mixed greens. For a dynamite stay-at-home night, chow down on one of Cuckoo's Nest's epic sandwiches and you won't be hungry for more. In fact, I challenge you to finish one without assistance.

Cactus Taqueria

5642 College Avenue at Shafter Avenue
658.6180
www.cactustaqueria.com
Open: M-Sat 11a-10p, Sun 11a-9p
$$ Vtn

This is the diet Mexican place. All the entrees are prepared super low-fat style, extra skin is taken off, fat dripped off, no lard in this place. The crispy chicken tacos are superb and the salsa here is some of the best around. When they say spicy they mean it! Two plates are more than enough to feed three mouths. Sip away on their house-made horchata (traditional and refreshing rice milk drink) while you are sauntering back to your pad.

It's Your Move Games and Hobbies

4920 Telegraph Avenue at 48th Street
547.4FUN (4386)
www.itsyourmovegames.com
Open: M 230-830p, Tu 1030a-1030p, Th-Sat 1030a-830p, Sun 1030a-630p

Everyone has a favorite game. For some it's held secret, for others they proclaim it to the world and enter championships to prove their might. Whatever your gaming fancy, this place has you covered. The traditional games of Scrabble, Chess, Monopoly and their friends are stacked next to new and interesting 3D puzzles, trivia teasers, city building games and ones where you are forced to communicate through humor or artistic strategy. The staff gaga about the games they sell. You can chill out and play from their used stack while lounging on a sofa in the store—talk about accommodating. They have a portable game section too, for traveling light, but not traveling bored.

Weekend

Fun activities for Saturdays and Sundays, plus yummy spots for brunch

Lois the Pie Queen, 60th Street

Weekends have a mood all their own. Laze around, relax with your loved ones or explore something new. Oaklanders like to get outside on the weekends. A short weekend getaway is a great time to see this city. Americans don't get nearly as much vacation time as allotted in some other countries, so take advantage of the weekends and kick back.

Lois the Pie Queen

851 60th Street at Adeline Street
658.5616
Open: M-F 8a-2p, Sat-Sun 7a-3p

Lois started cooking pies with her mother and grandmother for church bake sales back in the 20's. With a little help from friends and family, she brought her pies and other home cooking to us all with this restaurant. The Pie Queen, as her husband called her, passed her secrets down to her son, who operates this place much the way she did when Reggie Jackson used to chum with her over pork chops and coffee. No other Oakland eatery can claim being considered as a national landmark. No other restaurant makes grits this scrumptious. No other place has as true a sweet potato pie, or as good a breakfast bargain. Get it? Got it? Good.

Redwood Regional Park

7867 Redwood Road off Skyline Boulevard
562-PARK
www.ebparks.org/parks/redwood.htm

This park is a tangle of wooded trails and grassy knolls, perfect for a family kickball game or a weekend barbeque. Redwoods were planted here in this prime climate when many of the older growth had been felled for new homes. Thanks to the rethinking of construction industries at the turn of the last century, the redwoods remain here in the Oakland hills, at 100-year heights. There is plenty of wildlife to lookout for here as birds and small mammals come to drink from the creek that runs through the park. If you're not up for a hike or a game, just grab a blanket and a book and trade the cityscape for a breathtaking arboretum.

El Huarache Azteca

3842 International Boulevard at 38th Avenue
533.239
Open: Everyday 8a-9p

For yet another twist on Mexican, try the delicacies of the center of the country. Aztec-inspired poblanos, huaraches and hacoyos should be part of every Mexican lover's vocabulary. And since the prices are so low, why not also taste the sweets from Toluca and the gorditas from Que Retaro?

Jade Villa

800 Broadway at 7th Street
839.1688
Open: M-Th 930a-3p, 5-930p, F 930a-3p, 5-10p,
Sat 9a-3p, 5-10p, Sun 5-930p

Don't be disheartened when they answer the phone in Chinese, this huge dim sum place is where Chinatown locals eat. But that doesn't mean you'll be served some combination of unaccustomed animal parts. Most of the dishes here are recognizable, and Jade Villa specializes in seafood, not eye of newt. Fearlessly pick from the plethora of carts rolling by. Don't miss the steamed shrimp and leek dumplings or the sesame balls (sweet). Everything is made fresh. Jade Villa does so much business they keep an aquarium of live fish, crabs and lobsters. Lunch on weekends is busy, but to me that is part of the fun. Also, the dim sum menu is more limited on weekdays and evenings. It is a very efficient place, get there early and you'll have no problem getting served quickly. Remember to pace yourself, the carts just keep on coming, and when the dim sum is this good (it's one of the few Zagat rated restaurants in Chinatown), you just can't get enough. This is a success story for family-owned businesses in Oakland. It started small, and has retained the same family ownership and many of the original staff, for over 20 years.

Oakland Zoo

Knowland Park
9777 Golf Links Road off of Interstate 580 exit
632.9525
www.oaklandzoo.org
Open: Everyday 10a-4p

Roaming the eastern hills of Oakland are a flock of giraffes, a pride of lions and a small herd of buffalo. The Oakland Zoo, in Knowland Park, is a fun adventure that isn't as over-populated as other more famous zoos in California. The zoo is used primarily as a breeding center, and a place for reproductive research, so there are large, close-knit groups of animals that regularly interact with zookeepers, and thus provide a very interesting new look at the animal world.

Grasshopper

6317 College Avenue at Alcatraz Avenue
595.3557
www.grasshoppersake.com
Open: Tu-F 5-10p, F-Sat 5-11p with bar open until midnight,
Sun 5-10pm

For a snazzed-up sake drink, there's an outstanding selection of Japanese spirits at Grasshopper. Don't miss the sweet potato fries for a salty partner to any of their top-notch drinks. The bar is lively on weekends, and the décor makes you feel like you're in some chic hotel lobby.

Cam Huong

920 Webster Street at 8ᵗʰ Street
444.8880
Open: Everyday 7a-7p

This is a friendly Vietnamese hole-in-the-wall where a huge sandwich with BBQ pork, fresh cilantro, cucumbers, and sauce is just 2.50. The green jelly desserts are fabulous and very filling. Don't be afraid of the color—it is basically just rice, sugar and mung bean paste. This is my favorite place for a weekend snack in Chinatown.

Tanjia

4905 Telegraph Avenue at 48th Street
653.8691
www.tanjias.com
Open: Tu-Sun 5-1030p

For a full-throttle Moroccan experience, the five-course prix fixé at Tanjia should do the trick. The exquisite décor and live, nightly belly dancing, combined with the spiced traditional entrees, are a trip to the other side of the world.

Open Studios

Various Locations
Info: 845.2612
www.berkeleyartisans.com

Two weekends a year the whole city comes alive with art. Thanks in great part to the guiding light of ProArts (see Get Inspired chapter), there are free self-guided tours in every area of the city. East Bay Open Studios are occasional throughout the year, but the early summer weekends are the highlight and include more venues, more openings and thus more refreshments.

Jack London Farmers Market and Oakland Artisan Marketplace

Jack London Square
Info: 238.4948
www.oaklandculturalarts.org
Saturdays and Sundays 10a-4p

The Artisan Marketplace at Jack London's Farmer's Market is a trip. Stalls with handmade lotions that turn dry skin to silk, intermingle with booths of handmade belly-dancing costumes. Funky jewelry, paintings and clothing vendors line the Embarcadero, sometimes sprinkled by the refreshing ocean mists. Plenty of restaurants and food stands accompany the festivities, all brought together with an assortment of live music. The market makes Jack London Square more interesting to explore, so save this spot for your weekend.

Volunteer

Fun, quick and easy ways to help the city flourish

Build a Sensory Garden for the Blind

Location: Lakeside Park Gardens
Estimated Time: 2 hours
Contact: 763.1959

Jobs: Work with gardening experts and kind-hearted locals on a new fragrant garden project. Plant and maintain a fragrant, lakeside garden.

Expose Science and Space to Kids

Location: Chabot Space and Science Center
Estimated Time: 2-5 hours
Contact: 336.7414
volunteers@chabotspace.org
www.chabotspace.org

Jobs: Help out at the world-class planetarium, work with school groups on creative science projects and hands-on learning, assist with special events and more.

In-Kind Donations Help

Location: varies
Estimated Time: 3 hours
Contact: Rebuilding Together Oakland, 1111 Pine St, Suite A, at 11th Street
www.rebuildingtogetheroakland.org

Jobs: Assist workers at the central distribution center to prepare donation package.

Alta Bates Summit Asian Outreach Program

Location: Chinatown Street Fest, 10 block radius of Chinatown
Estimated Time: 2 hours
Contact: http://www.altabates.com/community/ao.html

Jobs: Help distribute health pamphlets and man a street booth with free blood pressure testing.

Help Repair Homes for the Elderly and Disabled

Location: Various
Estimated Time: 6 hours
Contact: Rebuilding Together Berkeley, 644.8979,
www.rebuildingtogetherabe.org

Jobs: Painting, tile work, plumbing, carpentry, and more. Both skilled tradespersons and novices are needed.

San Pablo Watershed Neighbors Education and Restoration Society

Location: El Sobrante Boys and Girls Club, 4660 Appian Way, El Sobrante
Estimated Time: 2 hours
Contact: 925.443.3925

Jobs: For those16 years and up. Get training on how to use global positioning systems to collect information about the creeks in Contra Costa County. Participate in actual surveys during the summer months. Work on the Golden Gate Spike Trail.

Help Protect and Heal the Community

Location: AIDS Volunteer Clearing House, 1904 Franklin St, Suite 211
Estimated Time: 2 hours
Contact: 419.3970

Jobs: Training to give out AIDS information and protection locally. Counselors, drivers, free clothing organizers, visitors, handymen, food bank help, therapeutic massager, and other services are always welcome.

Sort, Locate and Hand Out Food

Location: Alameda County Food Bank, sites may vary
Estimated Time: 2-4 hours
Contact: 635.3663, http://www.accfb.org/volunteer_signup.html

Jobs: Telephone, organizing food, planning drives, handing out food, office work—you choose your job.

Help out at a Domestic Violence Shelter

Location: A Safe Place Shelter, Oakland
Estimated Time: depends on your availability
Contact: 986.8600, programs@asafeplacedvs.org

Jobs: The entire staff are volunteers, so the work is varied. Office work, kitchen help, clean-up, telephone answering, and other services are greatly appreciated.

Berkeley Path Walkers

Location: various trails, paths and wilderness in the greater Berkeley area
Estimated Time: 2 hours
Contact: 540.7223, charlie_paths@comcast.net

Jobs: Build, restore and create pathways and trails outdoors, different levels of physical energy exerted.

Promote Literacy

Location: Bay Area Literacy, various locations
Estimated Time: 2-3 hours
Contact: 1.888.740.7323, www.literacynet.org/balit

Jobs: Help adult learners fill out job applications, read to their children, gain confidence and pass tests. Efficient teacher training given.

Backpack with Inner City Youth

Location: Big City Mountaineers, trip locations varies
Estimated Time: Requires at least a week-long commitment
Contact: www.bigcitymountaineers.org

Jobs: Leading groups of kids, hiking, and more. Training provided.

Cheer Up Hospitalized Kids

Location: Children's Hospital Oakland, 747 52nd Street
Estimated Time: Your actual volunteer time is what hours you set. It is a more involved process to become one of the hospital's trusted volunteers, but well worth it once you are in the system. There is a minimum 16- hour total commitment.
Contact: www.childrenshospitaloakland.org, click on *Ways to Help*, or fax: 597.7133

Jobs: The jobs vary greatly within the hospital, but center around promoting peace of mind for the children, and increasing their well-being.

Regional Park Projects

Location: Black Diamond Mines, Botanic Garden, Crab Cove, Tilden Park, Redwood Park, Coyote Hills, and more
Estimated Time: depends on your availability or type of work
Contact: 544.2515, volunteers@ebparks.org

Jobs: Earth Day events, trail days, trail maintenance and improvements, public safety, pruning, erosion control, coastal clean up, help with events like disabled youth fishing derbies and more.

Community Gardening Project

Location: Parks and Housing areas around the city
Estimated Time: From a few hours, to a weekly commitment
Contact: Gardening Project Coordinator, 238.2197

Jobs: Participate in horticulture workshops and learn while you help out in the city garden.

Special Event Volunteering

Location: Community buildings around the city
Contact: www.oaklandnet.com/oakshines

Jobs: Help with the annual Thanksgiving Dinner, Walk to School Day, Egg Hunt and other annual celebrations.

Community Compost and Gardening Program
Location: City Slicker Farms, located across the city
Estimated Time: A few hours, or make a longer commitment, whatever you choose
Contact: 763.4241

Jobs: Pick up compost from local households. Saturdays at Center Street Farm, corner of 16th and Center Streets, from 10am to 1 pm, there are weekly community gardening sessions.

Clean-Up Days
Locations: City-wide, during special days throughout the year
Estimated Time: One-day commitment
Contact: more info: www.keepoaklandbeautiful.org

Jobs: Help with Earth Day, Daffodil Day, Clear-a-drain Day, Creek-to-Bay Day, and Arbor Day.

Other Resources:

You can find fun and enriching ways to give back to the community. Great websites to connect with local volunteer opportunities are:

www.volunteerinfo.org
www.oaklandheros.org
www.openhand.org
www.volunteermatch.org
www.communityimpact.org
www.idealist.org
www.onebrick.org
www.oaklandnet.com/community/volunteers_all.htm

City for Free

The ultimate guide to free events, free admission, free films and more

Just as the saying goes, "the best things in life are free", so are most of the best things in Oakland—or they can be free if you know when to go. Even those without many financial choices can be a part of our rich cultural web. Music and art are the stuff of the soul. Nature abounds in the hills above Oakland, breathtaking views of the bay inspire the photographer in everyone. There are many adventures to be had without reaching for your wallet. I encourage everyone to try one day for free, bring a picnic and enjoy museums, open-air markets, parks, and summer concerts. The arts community is under constant financial threat due to our skewed priorities, if you can make a donation to art and music it will make life more livable for those who cannot and for future generations.

Outdoor Movies

Washington Street, between 9th and 10th Streets in Old Oakland
Info: 238.4734
www.filmoakland.com
www.oldoakland.org

Classic titles and summer blockbusters bring everyone together for these free summer showings. Bring lawn chairs and a picnic, or buy caramel corn from a sidewalk stand. Old Oakland is transformed into a cinema block party for everyone to enjoy.

Free Swims

Oakland Parks and Recreation City Pools
Nine locations citywide, open during the summer
Info: 238.2196

During national Parks and Recreation Month (July), one day at each of the nine City of Oakland pools is set aside for free recreational swim. All ages are welcome. The shallow end is marked off, and most of the pools have a deep end. The regular price is 2 dollars, so you can make a refreshing summer dip a habit.

Free Walking Tours

Wednesdays and Saturdays
Beginning Location: Frank H. Ogawa Plaza
Info: 238.3234
aallen@oaklandnet.com
http://www.oaklandnet.com/government/cmo/walkingTours/default.html

Explore different areas of the city for free with a knowledgeable guide. Custom tours can also be arranged. Make a reservation for a group. (See **Explore** chapter for more information.)

Noches de Verano

Outdoor Cinema Series in the Fruitvale District
Corner of 34th Avenue and East 12th Street, near Fruitvale BART
Evenings July through September

Free outdoor movies draw a crowd every weekend in the up-and-coming Fruitvale district. Snacks stands and taco trucks abound, just bring you family and a blanket or some lawn chairs and enjoy a plethora of good movies, all with Spanish subtitles.

Free Classical Concerts

St. Paul's Episcopal Church
114 Montecito Avenue at Bay Place
Info: 834.4314

Times and days vary, but the concerts usually begin at 4pm most Sundays. A variety of classical and vocal arrangements are performed. The members of the Oakland Civic Orchestra are regulars. The church is a peaceful setting to hear this beautiful music. Even if you don't normally listen to classical music, hearing it live can enhance your appreciation. Kids are welcomed. The harmonious chords have a very relaxing effect, a perfect weekend activity.

Free Wine Tasting

Farmstead Cheeses and Wines
At the Alameda Marketplace
1650 Park Street at Buena Vista Avenue, Alameda
864.WINE

Jeff Diamond, the owner of this store at Alameda Marketplace, has been a wine and cheese aficionado his whole life and is now sharing his worldly expertise with us. Each Saturday, holidays excepted, he uncorks a full course wine tasting, from the dry reds all the way to sweet whites and dessert wines. There are weekly specials on unique vintages. He'll even help you pair cheeses with each wine. I especially like the Three Sisters, a sharp Spanish cheese, and the Shropshire Blue, a brilliant gold and blue Stilton. There is no purchase requirement for the wine tasting, but it sure is hard to resist.

Free Chess Lessons

Lakeview Branch Library
550 El Embarcadero at Grand Avenue
238.7344
Every Wed & Sat 330-530p

Chess pro Demetrius Goins will work with anyone, no matter how bad you think you are, or what your age. Don't be afraid! This is the perfect opportunity to take your game to the next level. On nice days the group plays outside, with a beautiful view of Lake Merritt. This is a great activity for families.

Free Tools
5205 Telegraph Avenue at 51st Street
597.5089
http://www.oaklandlibrary.org/Branches/temtll.htm
Open: M 1230-8p, Tu 10a-530p, W-Th Closed, F 12-530p, Sat 10a-530p, Sun
Closed

The tool lending library is truly one of a kind. Borrow a set of wrenches or a concrete mixer, an electric saw or a shovel. I realize every traveler may not need these items, but it is interesting to know about anyway. There are over 2700 tools on hand. In order to use the facility you must have or know someone a current resident of Oakland, preferably one who already has a public library card. Who knows when you may need a tool next.

Free Teen Movie Night
Dimond Branch Library
3565 Fruitvale Avenue at MacArthur Boulevard
482.7844

Every August the Dimond Branch Library hosts movie nights, where teens can get together and watch funny films. It is a great way to meet new people, and give the parents a night alone, or at least a few hours out. There are different teen nights throughout the year at different Oakland library branches. Check their website for more up to date information.

Free Knitting and Crocheting Lessons and Clubs
Piedmont and Golden Gate Libraries
Sat 3-4p at Piedmont Library: 160 41st Street at Piedmont Avenue
F 330-530p Golden Gate: 5606 San Pablo Avenue at 56th Street

No library card is needed to join these free knitting and crocheting workshops. People of all ages and abilities gather with skilled knitters who help them learn new stitches and patterns. Just bring some yarn and needles, or a current project and chat it up while you work with your hands. This kind of circle has been held sacred in many cultures for centuries, as a community time that is also productive. It is genuinely fun and also very satisfying!

168 City for Free

Free Book Discussion Group

Golden Gate Branch Library
5606 San Pablo Avenue at 56th Street
Info and current title: 597.5023
Every 4th Tuesday, 630p

Go online to see what book the Golden Gate Library Club is currently reading. Pack it on the airplane to pass the time away. Then when you arrive you'll be ready to join in the discussion with locals about the book. Titles vary greatly, this book club is particularly diverse. There is also a teen book club on the second Monday of each month. No library card is needed and new visitors are always welcome.

A note about Oakland libraries: Even if you are not particularly struck with book clubs, the Oakland Library system is one of the best resources in this city. There are always pages of events listed on the main website from book readings with Isabelle Allende, to free knitting lessons, to workshops on diversity, to free homework tutoring. Whether you are living or moving here, or are on vacation, taking part in at least one library event will bring you a wonderful local flavor and learning experience.

Berkeley Art Museum

2626 Bancroft Avenue at College Avenue, Berkeley
642.0808
www.bampfa.berkeley.edu
Free: 1st Thursday of each month 11a-7p, including 530p screening at Pacific Film Archive across the street at 530p show!

See an art show in the unique structure of the BAM, designed so that one wall unfurls itself inside the building without corners or breaks. There is a great collection of permanent exhibits as well as traveling show. Cap off a day of art at the Pacific Film Archive, a museum annex. Head over to Intermezzo for a salad before the 5:30 screening.

Free French Classes

Temescal Library
5205 Telegraph at 52nd Street
Every other Friday, usually 1st and 3rd, call to be sure, 330-5p

These afternoon classes are a chance to learn a new tongue with other beginners. Not only are there many Spanish speakers in the Bay Area, but also many French speakers too. In fact there are two French bilingual schools to accommodate all their kids! French is a beautiful language. OK, I admit I am totally biased here. There is a whole new muscle in your brain just waiting to be flexed learning new words. Then you can go and impress Gregoire when you get take out, or get into a new culture with a linguistic understanding as well.

Oakland Museum of California

1000 Oak Street at 10th Street
238.2200
www.museumca.org
Free: 2nd Sunday of each month, noon-6

This is a real keystone for culture and science in California. It is everything a museum is should to be. (See **Explore** chapter for more museum information.)

Hikes

Hiking is always free!

There are hundreds of hikes in the Bay Area, and though I have included a few of them in the **Get Active** chapter, I would refer anyone interested in a more complete list to *East Bay Out*, a wonderful book by Malcolm Margolin that gives you all the possibilities in great detail.

More for Free

Yes, this is a guide to Oakland—and I know I've stretched it to some places (see **Nearby** *chapter) in Berkeley and Alameda too—but San Francisco? Yes, I had to include the museums there. When I lived in London I got used to having such easy entry—the museums are free or pay-what-you-can. This "high art" should be accessible to all. It is more than just beautiful objects, but expressions of humanity's ups and downs that can speak to all our senses. So even though the US has made many of these places of art and culture a luxury, these are the days and times when you can see it all for free. We should not forget that there are more than machines and mass media. Art is as necessary to life as these tools.*

Stern Grove Concerts
17th Street at Sloat Boulevard, San Francisco
Mid June thru the end of August
Sundays, 2p
Stern Grove Outdoor Amphitheater

The non-profit organization that hosts this yearly festival has been bringing world-class performing arts to the Bay Area for free since 1938. Need I say more? Each concert is a unique experience, and since it's free, why not attend as many as possible.

Yerba Buena Center for the Arts
701 Mission Boulevard 3rd Street, San Francisco
415.978.ARTS
www.ybca.org
Free: 1st Tuesday of each month

Modern art and resident artist exhibitions that always push the proverbial envelope.

Bay Area Discovery Museum
557 McReynolds Road, Sausalito
415.339.3900
http://www.baykidsmuseum.org/
Free: 2nd Saturday of each month 1-5p

An indoor/outdoor museum featuring hands-on exhibits of waves and tide pools and a theater for kids.

San Francisco Museum of Modern Art

151 3rd Street at Minna Street, San Francisco
415.357.4000
www.sfmoma.org
Free: 1st Tuesday of each month 11a-545p, half price every Thursday 6-845p

Elegant architecture with a bold stripe motif set the SFMOMA out from other buildings downtown. The extensive permanent collections of modern painting and photographs are always accompanied by several special exhibitions and installations. There is a new library and research center for talks and computer data base access.

De Young Museum

75 Tea Garden Way, Golden Gate Park, San Francisco
415.863.3330
www.deyoungmuseum.org
Free: 1st Tuesday of each month 930a-5p

A real smorgasbord of art and artifacts, people seem to have a love/hate relationship to the new and improved De Young. As for me, I love the building's architecture, and the Andy Goldsworthy entry. The collections are astoundingly diverse and really quite good. On the one hand it is interesting to see the ritual artifacts of Oceana in the gallery next to collodion photographs and Haitian paintings, or Oaxacan stone carvings around the corner from art glass and works of Jasper Johns. On the other hand there is little to no information about the artifacts; they are simply presented as art for arts sake, which may not respect the context in which the objects were produced, or their purpose. Back on the plus side, the observatory tower rewards museum goers with a great view all the way to the coast. The bi-monthly special exhibitions are very well done. I say all this not to steer anyone away, but to open conversation about how museums are curated and simply to take notes of the pros and cons of this innovative approach, which I think everyone will agree it is. Just pace yourself and plan for a tea break next door at the Japanese gardens afterward (which unfortunately have very rare free hours, usually in the early morning).

San Francisco Zoo

Sloat Boulevard at the Great Highway, San Francisco
415.753.7080
www.sfzoo.org
Free: 1st Wednesday of every month 10a-5p

One of this countries premier educational zoos, with special exhibits, birds and primate houses and snow leopards, my favorite! Fun for everyone.

Exploratorium

3601 Lyon Street at Jefferson Street, San Francisco
415.561.0360
www.exploratorium.edu
Free: 1st Wednesday of each month

An excellent playground for the sciences with hands-on exhibits that illustrate various physical principals. The Palace of Fine Arts, a wonderful outdoor pantheon and park is right next door.

Asian Art Museum

200 Larkin Street at Fulton Street, San Francisco
415.581.3500
www.asainart.org
Free: 1st Tuesday of each month 10a-5p

One of the best collections of Asian art in this country is in San Francisco, Organized by geographic region, the jade carvings, Japanese baskets and Indonesian puppets are special highlights.

The Legion of Honor

Lincoln Park, 34th Avenue at Clement Street, San Francisco
415.863.3330
www.thinker.org
Free: every Tuesday

With a huge Rodin sculpture collection, situated overlooking the Golden Gate and beyond, the Legion of Honor can't be missed on a trip to the Bay Area. Gothic and Renaissance art are coupled with new photography exhibits and a rich display of Baroque and Victorian furniture and paintings.

Cartoon Art Museum

655 Mission Street at New Montgomery Street, San Francisco
415.CAR.TOON
www.cartoonart.org
Free: 1st Tuesday of each month, 11a-5p

A one-of-a-kind museum of cartoon art including political cartoons, films, comic books, and prints. Exhibits can range from cartoons of gay and lesbian culture to the creepy, to commentary on the Middle East conflicts.

Lodge

Much of Oakland's hospitality industry is centered around the airport. Most are reasonably priced, and there is usually ample availability. Unique bed and breakfasts and more upscale hotels are closer to City Center. Camping, or planning through Educational Services are two cheaper and more authentic ways to experience this city. Surprisingly, many of the bed and breakfasts are cheaper than the chain hotels, but you may have to reserve them in advance because they have 4 rooms, instead of 304. I think more options will be available in the future, but here are a few current choices:

Bed-and-Breakfasts

Berkeley-Oakland Bed and Breakfast Network
547.6380
www.bbonline/ca/berkeley-oakland

Rose Garden Inn

2740 Telegraph Avenue at Ward Street, Berkeley
549.2145
www.rosegardeninn.com

Covered with creeping roses and trumpet vines, this beautiful estate has been transformed into a full-service bed-and-breakfast. A scrumptious breakfast buffet is served every morning. Most of the 40 rooms have fireplaces, which make it great for a romantic getaway. Free parking.

Bates House

399 Bellevue Avenue at Van Buren Avenue
893.3881
www.bateshouse.com
Rooms: 4
Price Range: $85-120

Dockside Boat and Bed

57 Clay Street at Embarcadero West
444.5858
www.boatandbed.com
Rooms: 8
Price Range: $125-400

Redwood House B&B

Redwood Heights (Oakland Hills)
Redwood Road across from Leona Heights Park
530.6840
Rooms: 2
Price Range: $80-120

The Hills B&B
Broadway Terrace (Oakland Hills) off of Highway 13
547.0652
Rooms: 1
Price Range: $100

A B&B on Fairmount On
640 Fairmount Avenue at El Dorado Avenue off of West MacArthur
Boulevard
653.7726
www.bbonline.com/ca/fairmount
Rooms: 3
Price Range: $70-95

Dean's B&B
480 Pedestrian Way at Claremont Avenue
652.5024
www.bbonline.com/ca/deans
Rooms: 2
Price Range: $80-85

Homestays

Educational Services International
www.edservintl.com
436.4848
Locations vary, but are all located near public transit

Top End Hotels

Claremont Resort and Spa

41 Tunnel Road off of Highway 13
800.551.7266
www.claremontresort.com
Rooms: 279
Price Range: $235-850

Hilton Hotel

1 Hegenberger Road at Doolittle Drive
800.774.1500
www.hilton.com
Rooms: 364
Price Range: $139-215

Waterfront Plaza Hotel

10 Washington Street at Water Street
800.729.3638
www.waterfrontplaza.com
Rooms: 144
Price Range: $195-400

Park Plaza Hotel

150 Hegenberger Road at Airport Access Road
800.635.5301
www.parkplazaoakland.com
Rooms: 190
Price Range: $119-206

Oakland Marriot

1001 Broadway at 10th Street
800.228.9290
www.marriot.com/oakdt
Rooms: 486
Price Range: $129-229

Airport Hotels

Holiday Inn Oakland Airport
500 Hegenberger Road at Edes Avenue
562.5311
www.holiday-inn.com/oaklandca
Rooms: 290
Price Range: $90-140

Best Western Inn and Suites
170 Hegenberger Loop at Hegenberger Road
633.0500
www.bestwestern.com
Rooms: 79
Price Range: $90-149

Days Inn Oakland Airport
8350 Edes Avenue at Enterprise Way
568.1880
www.daysinnoakland.com
Rooms: 142
Price Range: $99- 119

City Center Accommodations

Courtyard by Marriot
988 Broadway at 10th Street
625.8282
www.marriot.com/oakcd
Rooms: 162
Price Range: $139-215

Best Western Inn at the Square
233 Broadway at 2nd Street
452.4565
www.innatthesquare.com
Rooms: 100
Price Range: $99-139

Executive Inn and Suites

1755 Embarcadero East off of Nimitz Freeway at 12th Street exit
536.6633
www.executiveinnoakland.com
Rooms: 226
Price Range: $99-179

Homewood Suites

1103 Embarcadero East at 10th Avenue
663.2700
www.oaklandwaterfront.homewoodsuites.com
Rooms: 132
Price Range: $119-269

Regency Inn

3720 Telegraph Avenue at 37th Street
652.9800
www.oaklandregencyinn.com
Rooms: 21
Price Range: $50-65

Washington Inn

495 10th Street at 5th Avenue
452.1776
www.thewashingtoninn.com

Nearby Hostels

www.norcalhostels.org

Fisherman's Wharf

204 Bay Street at Stockton Street
Bldg. 240, Fort Mason
415.771.7277
$22 shared room, private available, breakfast included, WiFi and parking

San Francisco City Center

685 Ellis Street at Larkin Street
415.474.5721
$23 shared room, private available, newly remodeled, free WiFi

San Francisco Downtown
312 Mason Street at Geary Street
415.788.5604
$22 shared room, private available, free coffee and tea

Pigeon Point Lighthouse American Youth Hostel
Pescadero
210 Pigeon Point Road at Cabrillo Way
650.879.0633
$18 shared Room, private available, hot tub, free breakfast, free parking

Marin Headlands
Fort Barry Building 941, Sausalito
Field Road
415.331.2777
$20 shared room, 17 and under $10, private available, common room with fireplace and piano, free parking

Point Reyes
Off Limantour Road at Muddy Hollow Road
Pt Reyes National Seashore
415.663.8811
$16 shared room, 17 and under $10, private available, patio with BBQ, free parking

Sacramento
925 H Street at 9th Street, Sacramento
916.443.1691
$20 shared room, 17 and under $10, private available; Gold Rush era mansion

Camping

Chabot Family Campground
Redwood Road at Anthony Chabot Regional Park
636.1684
www.ebparks.org/parks/anchabot.htmSites: 75
Prices: $14-20

Nearby

Highlights from the nearby towns of Alameda and Berkeley

Sea Salt, San Pablo Avenue

Sea Salt
2512 San Pablo Avenue at Dwight Way, Berkeley
883.1720
www.seasaltrestaurant.com
Open: Everyday 1130a-10p
$$ Fr Ro

Every day of the week, between the hours of 4 and 6 pm, Sea Salt has 1-dollar oysters on the half shell. And these aren't just any oysters, they are flown in from the east and north, and taken from the waters of the California coast from small caring farmers. No poisons are introduced into the sea, no populations devastated, no bioengineered fish that could ruin marine health. Enjoy seafood without worry! The freshest, sustainably farmed seafood is served here in elegant and inventive ways. Lunch dishes are fairly expensive for the amount on the plate, but when you imagine how much trouble the kitchen goes through to insure that their fish are caught without harming the ecosystem, you realize how worthwhile it is. Dinner courses are sublime, the grilled calamari is outstanding, but you really can't go wrong when, come early Saturday night, you are filling up on divine oysters.

La Pena Cultural Center and Café Valparaiso
3105 Shattuck Avenue at Prince Street, Berkeley
Open: Hours vary depending on the show
Café Hours: Wed-Sat 9a-2p and 530-1030p, Sun 9a-930p
Administration and Box Office Hours: Tue-Fri 10a-5p

The tastes and sounds of Latin America are brought together under one roof at La Pena. Musical offerings, activist meetings, CD release parties and impassioned poetry light up the stage every night of the week. Check out something new and be ready to get your groove on. The café serves up harmonious accompaniments to all the tunes.

Auctions by the Bay

Warehouse Annex Auction House, Building 25, Alameda
740.0220
www.auctionsbythebay.com

Monthly auctions of antiques, collectibles and furniture are gathered together from local estates and elsewhere.

Rick and Ann's

2922 Domingo Avenue at Ashby Avenue, Berkeley
649.8538
rickandanns@sbcglobal.net
www.rickandanns.com
Open: Everyday 8a-230p, W-Sat 530-930p
$$ Vtn Fam

Tucked under the shadow of the gorgeous, if not domineering, Claremont Hotel is a small street of shops, the highlight of which is clearly Rick and Ann's. Their generous breakfast portions and sublime pancakes attract a line out the door on weekends. I like to go early on weekdays when the service is faster and the place isn't crowded. They use the freshest ingredients. Rick and Ann, a local couple, modeled this place after their own breakfast table. After filling my belly it is fun perusing the posh stores along the street, or buying a fresh loaf of bread from the organic bakery a few doors down.

Emeryville Bayside Walk

At the base of University Avenue follow path in either direction, Berkeley
http://www.berkeleypaths.org/walkhandouts/walk_EastshoreStatePark.htm

The newly renovated Bayside trail runs from Emeryville pier straight to Richmond, with plans for further expansion. The path has a larger paved section with a narrow dirt track for runners alongside. The paved track is smooth enough to rollerblade and draws many bikers as well. The *next* best thing to walking along the beach is surely walking right next to the water. If you're lucky you may spot a seal or a flock of pelicans. Some sections of the trail are accompanied by flowering gardens, others go through wet-land preserves on planks, still others play host to the best fetch ground for you and your furry friends.

Berkeley Pier Walk
Marina Drive, at the very end of University Avenue, Berkeley

The mile-long Berkeley pier was significantly shortened by the Loma Prieta quake in 1989, but is still a nice long walk to the end. With the bay waters on both sides, and Alcatraz, Angel Island and the Golden Gate straight out ahead, it is a great vantage point on a sunny day. Fisherman have been known to pull up small sharks and rays from these waters.

La Note
2377 Shattuck Avenue at Channing Way, Berkeley
843.1535
www.lanoterestaurant.com
Open: M-F 8a-230p, Sat-Sun 8a-3p, Th-Sat 6-10p
$$ Vtn S Fr

This eatery is a real taste of Provence, serving house made pastries until they run out. Get there early to make sure you get your pick. The simple croissants are some of the best I have had this side of the Atlantic; the almandine is also good. Lattes served in bowls pair perfectly with the fluffy-baked delights. In the spring and summer they open up the flower-covered back patio, my favorite spot to read and have time to myself. I have never had a bad dish here, so if you want more than a croissant and coffee, the eggs, salads, soups, gingerbread pancakes...everything is good.

Urban Ore Ecopark
900 Murray Street at Ashby Avenue, Berkeley
841.SAVE (7283)
Open: Sun 10a-7p, Mon-Sat 830a-7p

Urban Ore is a candy shop for anyone with a creative imagination. Try to picture an assortment of East Bay homes completely deconstructed and organized by item in a large indoor-outdoor warehouse. Stroll by the bathtub section and rendezvous at the toaster ovens or records. Isles of antique doors, mirrors and all possible forms of furniture make this one of the funnest places to shop. Pick up some found art and explore the depths of this recycled wonderland.

Alameda Marketplace

1650 Park Street at Buena Vista Avenue, Alameda
865.1500 (main grocery number)
Open: M-Sat 8a-8p, Sun 8a-7p

Alameda Marketplace brings together all sorts of high-quality local produce and groceries under one roof. This makes it easy to buy fresh sausage from the sausage maker, a wide array of cheese and wine from a true connoisseur, bread from a baker, you get the idea. The people who work the stands in this market really care about what they are selling, how it is made, where is comes from and that it is of the highest quality possible.

Le Bateau Ivre

2629 Telegraph Avenue at Carleton Street, Berkeley
849.1100
hello@lebateauivre.net
www.lebateauivre.net
Open: Tu-Sun 9a-230p, Tu-Th & Sun 5-930p, F-Sat 5-1030p
$$ Vtn S Fr WiFi

Another great breakfast spot is Le Bateau Ivre, or drunken boat in old French. (If you are trying to say you are drunk in French, don't say *je suis ivre*, it won't make any sense to a modern Frenchman, try *je suis cramé* instead). The scones are made in house. Breakfast is inexpensive and elegant, though the service can be very slow. This restaurant is in a historic house, and few changes have been made to the building. It really feels like a home. Classical music trickles around the cozy lace-covered tables that are scattered through rooms with window seats and fireplaces. It's a great study spot where few other students loiter. The waiters don't make you feel as though you've outstayed your welcome—I've spent hours writing there. Be forewarned however, this is not a good place to go in a rush, because it employs all the European traits, namely eating out as an event not to be done in a hurry. Try not to get impatient; just slow down and plan to stay a while.

Berkeley International Food Festival

Info: 845.4106
www.berkeleyinternationalfoofestival.com
University and San Pablo Avenues
Noon-6, last weekend in April annually

Peruse the vibrant booths at this yearly fair. So many cuisines and cultures are represented that it is impossible to choose where to eat. Try anything and everything. They have Jamaican, Indian, Pakistani, Iranian, Spanish, Thai, Hawaiian foods... the list goes on. There are family recipes and cooking demonstrations throughout the day. Games and activities are in full swing as a part of this food celebration. Three stages are set up with international musicians from California Bluegrass to a Balinese orchestra. It's all in the mix.

Stone Mountain and Daughter

2518 Shattuck Avenue at Dwight Way, Berkeley
Berkeley
845.6106
www.stonemountainfabric.com
Open: M-F 10a-630p, Sat 10a-6p, Sun 11a-530p

Whether you are just learning to sew, or you are an experienced quilter or seamstress, Stone Mountain can accommodate. With an extensive sale section, a glittering wall of buttons, yarns and unique fabrics, this woman-owned business has been a treasure chest for creativity for over 25 years.

Trader Vic's

9 Anchor Drive at Powell Street, Emeryville
653.3400
Info: trvics@aol.com
Open: Everyday 1130a-11p
$$$ Fam Vtn R

A Bay Area classic, Vic went to Tahiti in 1937 and came back with a slew of new and unique recipes no one had tasted on these shores. He started the trend of America's foreign appetite, as well as in inventing the Mai Tai, and serving my uncle his first legal drink at 21.

Berkeley Bowl

2020 Oregon Street at Shattuck Avenue, Berkeley
843.6929
www.berkeleybowl.com
Open: M-Sat 9a-8p, Sun 10a-6p

Create any dish from a slew cultural tradition from the vast array of ingredients housed in this recycled building. Once a bowling ally, Berkeley Bowl was revamped and restructured with energy-efficient, green building materials, and is now one of the largest independent super markets around. The vegetable and fruit section are not to be missed; I have never seen an assemblage that could compare. Early in the week when they get new shipments of flowers the old ones go on sale. I have found barely-bruised tuberoses and lilies for 1.99 a bunch. In short, Berkeley Bowl arms chefs from any nation, and also cheaply feeds my penchant for ikebana. Steel yourself as the crowds can make it seem like Beijing at rush hour.

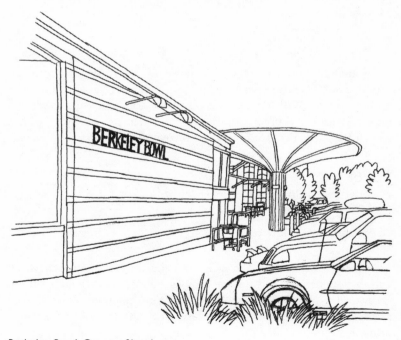

Berkeley Bowl, Oregon Street

Baubles and Beads

1676 Shattuck Avenue at Cedar Street, Berkeley
644.BEAD
www.baublesandbeads.com
Open: M-Sat 1030a-630p, Sun 11a-5p

It is easy to get lost in this array of glass, semiprecious stones and beads from all over the world. It can add up quick when you put all the findings and beads together, but the talented staff can help you successfully design any kind of jewelry, they even have tools for you to use in-store. February there is a trunk show where the prices dip substantially, and each month there is a 30% discount on whatever semiprecious stone they want to trim down on. Take a class if you want to learn wire wrapping or some other design technique. (See **Learn** chapter for more information.)

Intermezzo

2442 Telegraph Avenue at Dwight Way, Berkeley
849.4592
Open: Everyday 8a-10p
$ Vn Vtn Fr S

I like large, satisfying bowls, full of organic greens. There has to be something crunchy, something sweet, and something salty. Intermezzo has mastered the salad—a huge pile of lettuces, half an avocado, a hard-boiled egg, cucumbers, chickpeas, kidney beans and an unparalleled poppy seed dressing that adds just the right amount of sweet. A piece of melon and a hearty slice of honey whole wheat bread made in house come along side. The price tag remains under 6 dollars. Of all the times I have eaten here I have never finished the whole salad.

Spring Plant Sales

Regional Parks Botanical Garden
Tilden Park, Wildcat Canyon Road
841.8732
www.nativeplants.org
Open: Sat 10a-3p

Buy California native plants to make your own garden, or just go to schmooze about horticulture and get wise advice and refreshments.

Chez Panisse

1517 Shattuck Avenue at Vine Street, Berkeley
548.5525
www.chezpanisse.com
Café: M-Th 1130a-3p & 530-1030p, F-Sat 1130a-330p &
5-1130p
Downstairs: M-Sat 6-630p & 830-930p (reservations required)
$$$ R Ro Vtn

Alice Waters and her famous Chez Panisse are known across
oceans for fostering sustainable farming techniques while serving
world class cuisine. In the more fancy downstairs the menu is fixed,
and costs between 65 and 85 dollars per person for three courses
without wine. Monday nights are 50. The waiting list can be
months long. All the produce comes from local organic farms, as
well as the meat, poultry and fish.

Waters has even started a foundation to promote sustainable
agriculture at all levels of food production. The chefs she
employees are a breed of their own, and when they move on they
usually start their own sustainable restaurant or bakery. Many of my
favorite places to eat in Oakland trace their roots to Chez Panisse
influence. If you have the bucks, and the foresight to make an
advance reservation, and don't mind a bit of snobbery, Chez
Panisse offers an unforgettable experience. Go upstairs for a menu
you can choose from, and slightly cheaper dishes.

The Jazz School

2087 Addison Street at Shattuck Avenue, Berkeley
845.5373
www.jazzschool.com
Concerts F-Sun, times and dates vary

The Jazz School top-notch jazz in an intimate setting,
complete with a jazz café that serves dinner and drinks during
shows. Space is limited; big names sell out fast. Tickets are very
cheap, so this is a great way to get wind of real jazz music without
shelling out too many bucks.

Bladium

800 West Tower Avenue at Lexington Street, Building 40, Alameda
814.4999
www.bladium.com
Open: M-F 5a-1130p, Sat-Sun 7a-10p

Bladium brings lacrosse to the West coast! They also have leagues for inline hockey, and soccer and a complete gym, with fitness equipment and a climbing wall. Teams and classes are offered throughout the year.

Wilderness Exchange

1407 San Pablo Avenue at Camelia Street, Berkeley
525.1255
Open: Sun-W 11a-7p, Th-Sat 10a-8p

For discount backpacking gear, used equipment, and honest advice on how to thoroughly enjoy the great outdoors, this is your place.

Marmot Mountain Works

3049 Adeline Street at Ashby Avenue, Berkeley
849.0735
www.marmotmountain.com/store-berkeley.htm
Open: M, Th, F 10a-8p, Tu-W Sat 10a-6p, Sun 11a-5p

Specialty extreme sports gear of the finest quality, sold by outdoor aficionados who really know their stuff make Marmot a fun and inspiring place to browse.

Ironworks

800 Potter Street at 6th Street, Berkeley
981.9900
www.touchstoneclimbing.com/bi.html
Open: MWF 6a-10p, Tu-Th 6a-11p, Sat-Sun 9a-8p

Indoor top rope climbing, lead climbing and bouldering facilites are open to those who pass the belay test. Classes and clinics are offered for all levels. Ironworks is where East Bay climbers congregate. They have a full gym and fitness services, including personal trainers, yoga, kickboxing and cardio workout sessions. Take five in the changing room saunas.

Frank Bette Center for the Arts

1601 Paru Street at Lincoln Street, Alameda
523.6957
www.frankbettecenter.org
Open: W-Sat 11a-7p, Sun 11a-5p

Born of the handwritten will of local artist Frank Bette, the Bette Art Center host readings, workshops and regular shows that display the rich creative talent of this area of the world. There are activities for all ages.

Albatross

1822 San Pablo Avenue at Delaware Street, Berkeley
the.bird (843.2473)
Open: Sun-Tu 6p-2a, W-Sat 430p-2a

Have you ever had that daydream of daydreams, where all your friends are hanging out together, playing darts and piles of pointless board games, armed with an endless supply of popcorn and microbrews? Albatross brings this dream to reality. Friends can crowd around comfortable tables and nooks and challenge themselves with Connect Four and Pictionary 'til the wee hours. Get a twenty-five cent bowl of popcorn and refill it as many times as you like for the rest of the night. The cherry on top—sometimes they even have live music.

Juan's Place

941 Carleton Street at 7th Street, Berkeley
845-6904
Open: M-F 11a-10p, Sat-Sun 2-10p
$ Fr Fam

Going to Juan's Place is like being invited to a party in Mexico. The atmosphere is always on the upswing, and so are the fish tacos. Quite honestly, they are the best I have ever had. The portions are huge, which makes the prices slightly higher than at other Mexican joints, but it is well worth it. This is where the cops eat, which I always take as a good sign.

Elmwood Videots

2988 College Avenue at Ashby Avenue, Berkeley
540.0222
Open: Everyday Noon-10p

No, it is not Video TS, it's Videots, like the extremely movie savvy employees who work there. As any local video store should have, there's an employee pick section that well out-does others of its kind. Lots of titles in DVD or VHS, organized in many ways that make them easy to find. Special deals include prepaid credits, Monday-through-Wednesday 2 for 1 rentals and on Sunday the 2nd title is 1 buck. Most rentals are five days. If you can't find that obscure film that you've been dying to see then jot it down in the suggestion book and they will get it for you. I got the Irish comedy series Father Ted, available no other place in the Bay Area.

Thai Buffet

Thai Buddhist Temple
911 Russell Street at Martin Luther King Jr. Boulevard, Berkeley
Open: Sundays 10a-2p
$ Fr Vtn

Sunday mornings a slew of colorful people flock to the Thai Buddhist Temple for some of the best, most authentic Thai food around. Several generations of women rise in the wee hours to cook curries and stews, soups and fried chicken, sticky rice and plantains, enough for the masses. Get in the token line first, to change your money into thin aluminum chips, so the servers don't have to touch the money. Then head to one of the many lines—it is hard to choose between the soup line and the papaya salad line, or the meat line, or the vegetable curry line. Don't miss the green curry with the straw mushrooms and butternut squash in the vegetarian line. If you have a sweet tooth get the Thai ice tea and the black sticky rice with fresh mangos. This Thai buffet is as close as California gets to a bustling Bangkok market. The money goes to the Buddhist temple to support the peaceful monks and their community.

Saul's Restaurant and Delicatessen

1475 Shattuck Avenue at Vine Street, Berkeley
848.3354
www.saulsdeli.com
Open: M-Th 8a-9p, F-Sat 8a-930p

Saul's is a great place to boot up. There are comfy booths to stretch out in, and homemade pickles on every table to munch on while you wait. If you haven't ever tried white fish salad, I highly recommend Saul's for your virginal experience with it–it is my favorite dish here. The smoky taste is divine and the protein gives you good energy The Rueben sandwiches and matzo ball soup also rank high, as do the rugelach, a classic Jewish cookie. On weekends it gets too busy too relax, I like going for an early dinner. Although Saul's cooks up good Jewish grub, it is not a kosher restaurant. The beef brisket is Neiman Ranch, from happy cows. This is where my mom and I go for our long talks.

Brennan's

720 University Avenue at 4th Street, Berkeley
841.0960
Open: Sun-Wed 11a-930p, Th-Sat 11a-1030p
(Bar open till 11pm)
$ Fam S

How could I not include Brennan's, even though it is not in Oakland, it vies for the top meat place with Everett and Jones (see **Casual Night Out** chapter). Brennan's has the most authentic Irish appeal of any place in the Bay Area. It offers pure meat and potatoes, and Irish coffee too. The best thing to grab from the buffet-style cafeteria line is the old-fashioned corned beef plate that comes with delicious boiled cabbage and gravy-doused mashed potatoes. It is the ultimate in comfort food, in a totally relaxed atmosphere. The meats are very high quality, and slow simmered au jus. There are tons of tables, and always room for the whole family, and the whole next-door neighbor's family, even on weekends. Come sit in a cozy corner, dig into a juicy brisket sandwich and watch Barry Bonds hit another foul ball.

Index

511, 20
À Côté, 88
AC Transit, 19, 22
    Transfer, 19
Air Lounge, 85
Airport, 18, 178
Alameda Marketplace, 186
Albatross, 192
Alley, 136
Arizmendi, 58, 59
Ashkenaz Dance Center, 116
Astronomy, 34
Athletics Baseball, 137
Auctions by the Bay, 184
B, 60
Backpacking, 160, 191
Bakesale Betty, 55
Barney's Gourmet Hamburger,
    53
BART, 21, 36, 37, 40, 75, 87, 134
Baubles and Beads, 189
Bay Area Bikes, 120
Bay Bridge, 19
Bay Wolf, 88
Bed and Breakfasts, 175
    Bates House, 175
    Dean's, 176
    Dockside Boat and Bed, 175
    On Fairmount, 176
    Redwood House, 175
    Rose Garden Inn, 175
    The Hills, 176
Berkeley Bowl, 188
Biking, 18, 21, 34, 120
Bladium, 191
Books
    Diesel, 129
    Pendragon, 128
    Sagrada Sacred Arts, 129
    Walden Pond Books, 126
Boys and Girls Club, 159
Brennan's, 194
Buses, Bus Transfers, 19
Cactus Taqueria, 151

Café Van Kleef, 75
Caffé 817, 53
Calendar, 30
Cam Huong, 155
Cameras
    Walter Bennett, 102
Camping, 180
Camron-Stanford House, 111
Capoeira, 115
Carnival, 36
Cato's Ale House, 63
Chez Panisse, 190
Children's Fairyland, 43, 104, 105
Chinatown
    Street Fest, 158
Chinese New Year's Bazaar, 31
Christopher's Burger, 54
CircusFit, 39
Citron, 89
Classes
    Art, 113
    Beading and Metal Work,
        114
    Capoeira, 115
    Chess, 166
    Crocheting, 167
    Dance, 116
    French, 169
    Iaido, 115
    Knitting, 114
    Music, 116
    Red Cross, 117
    Sewing, 115
    Swimming, 117
    Yoga, 123
Cleveland Cascade, 123
Climate, 7
Club Anton, 80
Cohen-Bray House, 111
Comedy, 81
Concerts, 38, 166
    Four Seasons, 80
    Redwoods, 41
    Stern Grove, 170

Woodminster, 80
County Fair, 37
CPR Preparedness Day, 32
Cuckoo's Nest, 150
Cultural Centers
    Asian, 116
    La Pena, 183
Cultural Crossroads, 126
Currency, 27
Customs, 26
Deep Roots Urban Teahouse, 66
Di Bartolo Restaurant, 89
Discount Fabrics, 100
Domestic Violence Shelter, 160
Dona Tomas, 70
Dunsmuir House, 33, 36, 38, 44,
    109
Earth Day, 33
East Bay Regional Parks, 3
Easter, 33
Educational Services
    International, 176
Egg Shop, 50
El Huarache Azteca, 154
Electricity, 27
Eli's Mile High Club, 79
Emergency, 26, 28, 29
Emery-Go-Round, 19
Entrez! Open House, 126
Everett and Jones BBQ, 75
Farmers Markets
    Jack London Square, 156
    Old Oakland, 25, 50
Fenton's Creamery, 64
Ferry, 22
Festivals
    African American, 31
    Art and Soul, 40
    Berkeley International Food,
        187
    Chinatown Streetfest, 40
    Chinese New Year, 31
    Cinco de Mayo, 34
    Dia de Los Muertos, 44
    Greek, 35
    Highland Games, 38
    Himalayan, 35
    Indigenous Peoples Day, 42
    International Films, 41
    Jewish Music, 32
    Juneteenth, 36

Laurel World Music, 39
Lunar New Year, 31
Montclair, 39
Moon Viewing, 43
Mother of the Year, 34
Noches de Verano, 165
Play Day on the Plaza, 37
Sistahs Steppin' in Pride, 40
Tet, 31
Tree Lighting Ceremony, 44
Fleet Week Cruise, 42
Flints Bar-B-Q, 71
Flowers by Myrna, 99
Food Bank, 159
Foreign Language Assistance,
    26
Full House, 48
Galleries
    Association of Clay and
        Glass Artists, 94
    Black Dot, 99
    Craft and Cultural Arts, 94
    Frank Bette Center, 192
    Joyce Gordon, 95
    Monart, 114
    Oakland ART, 94
    Oakland Art Murmur, 96
    Open Studios, 156
    Pro Arts, 96
    Rock Paper Scissors, 100, 114
    Studio One, 113
    Thelma Harris, 94
Games and Hobbies, 151
Gardens
    Community, 161, 162
    Japanese, 111
    Lakeside Park, 158
    Morcom Rose, 108
    Tilden, 113
Genova Delicatessen, 57
Golden Gate Fields Racetrack,
    137
Golden Lotus, 56
Gondola Servizio, 110
Grand Bakery, 131
Grand Lake Theater, 41, 69, 74
Grasshopper, 155
Gregoire, 149
Greyhound, 20
Hank and Frank, 120
Heartfelt, 128

Heinold's First and Last Chance
    Saloon, 110
History, 2
Holy Land, 55
Homestays, 176
Hospitals, 161
    Highland, 29
Hostels, 179
Hotels, 177, 178
    Best Western Inn, 178
    Best Western Inn and Suites,
        178
    Claremont Resort and Spa,
        177
    Courtyard by Marriot, 178
    Days Inn, 178
    Executive Inn and Suites, 179
    Hilton, 177
    Holiday Inn, 178
    Homewood Suites, 179
    Oakland Marriot, 177
    Park Plaza, 177
    Regency Inn, 179
    Washington Inn, 179
    Waterfront Plaza, 177
House of Chicken and Waffles,
    140
IB's, 60
Ice Skating, 123
Intermezzo, 189
International Visitors, 26
Ironworks, 191
Jack London Square, 32, 33, 34,
    36, 38, 42, 43, 44, 75, 79, 83,
    140, 156
Jade Villa, 154
Jazz School, 190
Jesso's, 73
Juan's Place, 192
Kayaking, 117
Key
    Company, xv
    Price, xv
    Service and Practicality, xv
Kimball's Carnival, 140
Knitting, 33, 99
    Article Pract, 100
    The Knitting Basket, 99
Koryo Wooden Charcoal B.B.Q.,
    74
Kosher, 55, 130, 131

La Note, 185
La Taza de Café, 81
Lacis, 101
Lake Merritt, 43, 49, 69, 110, 111,
    117, 123
L'Amyx Tea Bar, 66
Lanesplitter Pizza, 139
Le Bateau Ivre, 186
Le Bonbon, 130
Le Cheval, 57
Legendary Palace, 139
Libraries
    African American, 93
    Dimond Branch, 167
    Golden Gate, 168
    Lakeview, 166
    Rockridge, 102
    Temescal, 169
    Tool Lending, 167
Lois the Pie Queen, 153
Los Comales, 59
Luka's Tap Room, 85
Lulu Rae Confections, 144
Mama Buzz Café, 66
Mama's Royal Café, 47
Maps, 8
    Dimond and Laurel, 16
    Downtown, Chinatown and
        Jack London Square, 10
    East Bay and Oakland, 9
    Fruitvale, 17
    Grand and Lakeshore, 11
    Montclair, 15
    Piedmont, 12
    Rockridge, 14
    San Francisco Bay Area, 8
    Temescal, 13
Maribel, 127
Marmot Mountain Works, 191
Martin Luther King Jr., 30
Meadows, 127
Mexicali Rose, 141
Mi Grullense Taco Truck, 54
Michael Mischer Chocolates,
    143
Mijori, 74
Mimosa Café, 71
Montclair Bistro, 88
Montclair Sports, 121
Movies, 69, 167
    Black Filmworks, 41

On Screen In Oakland, 70
Outdoor, 39, 165
Museums
    African American, 93
    Asian Art, 172
    Bay Area Discovery, 170
    Berkeley Art, 168
    Cartoon Art, 173
    Chabot Space and Science
        Center, 106, 158
    De Young, 171
    Ebony Art, 96
    Exploratorium, 172
    Legion of Honor, 172
    Mills College Art, 95
    MOCHA, 95
    Oakland, 31, 32, 35, 41, 92,
        93, 169
    San Francisco Modern Art,
        171
    Western Aerospace, 108
    Yerba Buena Center for the
        Arts, 170
Nail Shop, 145
Nailphoria, 145
Neldam's Danish Bakery, 125
New World Vegetarian, 76
Newspapers
    East Bay Express, 30
    Tribune, 5, 30, 49
Nomad Café, 63
Oakland Police, 29
Oliveto, 72, 86
Parades, 37
    Black Cowboys, 42
    Haunted Harbor, 43
    Lighted Yachts, 44
    United Nations, 42
Pardee Home, 105
Parks, 161
    East Bay Regional, 107
    Huckleberry Botanic
        Preserve, 107
    Redwood Regional, 153
    Roberts Recreation Area, 120
    Sibley Volcanic Reserve, 107
    Tilden, 107, 113
Pearl Oyster Bar, 90
Peralta Hacienda, 109
Phnom Penh House, 57
Pho Hoa Lao, 146

Piedmont Lane Antiques, 129
Piedmont Stationers, 101
Pimlico Place, 127
Pizzaiolo, 73
Pools, 165
    Lions, 119
    Temescal, 119
Poppy Fabrics, 102
Preservation Park, 108, 109
Prism Café, 65
Pro Arts, 96
Purple Pepper Pizza, 150
Raiders, 137
Red Cross, 117
Resources, 162
Rick and Ann's, 184
Rockridge Café, 48
Ruby Room, 80
Running, 37, 121
Sailing
    Strictly Sail Pacific, 33
    Tall Ship Expo, 32
Saul's Restaurant and
    Delicatessen, 194
Sea Salt, 183
See Jane Run, 121
Shopping Districts, 132
Silkroad Fabric, 99
Snapshot Mosaics, 101
Spas
    Au Natural, 145
    Nola's Skin Care Boutique,
        144
Spring Plant Sales, 189
Spud's Pizza, 63
Stone Mountain and Daughter,
    187
Stork Club, 140
Swan's Market, 125
Sweet Adeline Bakeshop, 143
Tamarindo Antojeria Mexicana,
    56
Tanjia, 156
Telescopes, 25
Temescal Café, 47, 81
Thai Buddhist Temple, Buffet, 193
Theaters
    Calvin Simmons, 81
    Fox, 6
    Grand Lake, 24, 41, 69
    Herbst, 81

Paramount, 83
Parkway, 64
TJ's Gingerbread House, 87
Tourettes Without Regrets, 79
Trader Vic's, 187
Trains, 19, 50, 107
    Amtrak, 19
    Caltrains, 19
Transit Information, 18, 20
Travel Insurance, 26
Travel Tips, xvi
Uncle Willie's Bar-BQ and Fish, 59
Universoul Circus, 42
Urban Ore Ecopark, 185
USS Potomac, 34, 42, 110
Video Rentals
    Global Entertainment, 149

Videots, 193
Volunteering, 30, 40, 160, 161
Walking, 36, 49, 108, 160, 165,
    169, 184, 185
Warriors, 137
Wheels of Justice, 120
White Elephant Sale, 32
White Horse Inn, 136
WiFi, xv
Wilderness Exchange, 191
Wines, 36, 41, 128, 166
World Cup Coffee Tamales, 60
XOX Truffles, 144
Yoshi's, 83
Zoo, 43, 155, 172
Zza's Trattoria, 149

Our Bios

Serena Bartlett

Founder, Author and grower of green beans

Having lived and traveled in over 20 countries, Serena has never had an easy time answering the question, "Where are you from?" She earned her degree from Friends World College and Long Island University. As a freelance writer, she is passionate about living, breathing cities that pulse with creativity and undercurrents of action and motion. Her escapades include romps on the Croatian shoreline, writing wine reviews in Lyon, teaching the hula to a retirement community in Kyoto, living and loving London, and getting lost many many times.

Daniel Ling

Creative Director, Illustrator, and maker of tea

Daniel is a graduate of UC Berkeley in Anthropology and an Oakland native. His artistic talent has surfaced in everything he has put his hand to; he especially enjoys designing t-shirts and logos for local organizations, including the swim team he coaches. His travels have always been documented in notebooks of his eloquent, often comedic sketches. Some of his unique finds will be documented in his upcoming book GrassRoutes Kids USA. He is a wise intermediary between the realm of creative freedom and that of technological innovation.